THE GREAT TRIBULATION

THE GREAT TRIBULATION

JAMES BARRINGTON-WHYTE

NEW HORIZON

ISBN 0 86116 746 5

Printed and Published by
NEW HORIZON (Transeuros Limited)
BOGNOR REGIS
GREAT BRITAIN

PREFACE

In a certain part of Holy Writ, we learn that it was the faith of a humble Roman soldier which received the greatest credit from our Lord. In the assertion of the obscure soldier of Louvain, spoken on that day when the Allied cause was in jeopardy, we have a like message for war as well as peace. His words so encouraged his fellows, that they were never forgotten, and were often quoted in barrack-rooms and camps in England, during the years of waiting for the Second Front; and hence form the theme of this book.

The following story concerns a number of "little people", who like thousands of others did not become famous, but who, whether on battlefield or at home, played a part in a cause, which often in their case had a higher significance than they could understand, at least at the time.

Someone may ask, "Seeing so many characters appear in the story who is the hero?" The answer is simply "None", except it be Almighty God Himself, who gives any success we may deserve. Those named would have wished me to show them playing their parts just they happened, all equally important; and that I have endeavoured to do.

I have, however, altered the story at certain points from the way it took place for two reasons; first, to hide the identities of the characters (all are true), and secondly, to fully bring out the theme of the story.

With this I dedicate it to the glory of God, and to all who in every nation fight for right with a pure conscience.

James Barrington-Whyte.

Chapter One

"For my money this so called Northern hospitality leaves a lot to be desired. Four long months we've been here now, and not a soul in the district'll do more than mutter a curt 'good evening'."

The speaker was a lean, bean-pole of a cockney lad, and he spoke with more than a little venom.

The scene was the austere inside of a wartime nissen hut lost in the heart-land of a snug Yorkshire village.

The time was the Fall of 1943...

"I kid you not," he continued to sound off, "when we left the South to come up here, all you North Country yobbos filled us with great stories about how you entertain. It's all lies; Wiltshire, or Norfolk, to name but two, were far better places to be stationed in."

He looked around, measuring the effects of his provocative statement on his audience. The obvious undercurrent of challenge was answered by a chorus of grunts and oaths from all corners of the hut.

"In other words, Hilton," said a stockily built soldier from the other end of the hut, "you're a Londoner, and we all know you cockneys think the world begins and ends in London."

"You're dead right, it does." Hilton's face broke into a lopsided grin... "Blitz, or no blitz, you can't beat the Old Smoke."

"Aw come off it." said the stocky one called Cragg, "From the very first week we arrived I've been O.K. You see I met a bloke and his wife in a pub in York, and they took me to their home in Bootham. Now I go there whenever the fancy takes me."

"Is that a fact?" said Hilton through his teeth, and with more than a touch of sarcasm. "Could it have anything to do with the fact that you come from the North – eh? It's very funny that I've been to a good many pubs in York, and around here for that matter, and no one's taken me under their wing. If you ask me this war's

1

been going on far too long; I'm fed up to the teeth."

During the course of this heated exchange the remainder of the hut had been engaged in feverish activity. A number were busy polishing kit for next morning's drill parade. Still more, mostly from other huts, were huddled in a corner, making up a card school.

As for the remainder they were sitting on the floor around a half completed model of an enormous dolls' house, which was due for early completion in order to coincide with the birthday of the young daughter of one of their number.

The making of all sorts and shapes of models had become a way of life during the terrible anti-climactic days of the waiting years culminating in the long promised Second Front.

Accordingly, many soldiers during their spare moments, went 'on production' to coin the phrase prevalent at the time.

Consequently it became a race against time to produce models of trains, scooters, ducks, and all the other characters dear to the hearts of children.

When completed these items were lovingly stowed away in lockers and kit-bags till leave time came around, when they were taken home as a surprise for some small family member.

In the unit which concerns this narrative, this particular dolls' house was considered by the 'Old Sweats' to be far and away the best piece of workmanship undertaken for a very long time.

"So you're browned off Hilton, my heart bleeds for you." said one of the men gathered around the model. "For your information you're not the only one, we all are. How could we be anything else? Unlike you however, I'm not a regular soldier, and therefore have even more reason to moan. Nevertheless I still intend to do my bit for the Old Country."

"Oh yeah." sneered Hilton, "a fat lot of good you're doing England by sitting on your fat buttocks making dolls' houses, Rattray old lad; you'll hardly beat Hitler that way."

"Moaning won't either," said Rattray. "I joined

up to pull my weight, and I'll do just that with a good heart. Why do you think Phelps and I, and many others, have gone 'on production' if it wasn't an outlet for some other activity, apart from brooding about this useless war. Ain't that right?" he poked his helper in the ribs.

"Dead right," muttered Phelps, who in his turn went on to point out that although he was basically a regular soldier, he'd lost all interest in Hitler, the war, and even the Army. Even so, if the war were to end the next day, and he was lucky enough to effect an early discharge, he'd refuse to go home till he'd completed the dolls house.

At this the whole hut tittered, for they were well aware that given half a chance Phelps would be back in civvy street long before the last shot was fired.

Another soldier who'd been busy polishing the brasses of his web-belt now joined the conversation.

"Good on yer mate, it does a fella good to hear the old battle between North and South; keep it up lads, we're all sure to win."

"We'll win if we don't lose, Grayson old hand," laughed Hilton. "What made you join the Army then?"

"To do my bit, of course; to be with the rest, even in the front line. That's why, there's nothing unusual about that."

"Good for you; I really admire that. You don't let religion keep you out of it, like some people I know," said Phelps slyly, tacking on the roof of the dolls' house with deliberate care.

By the evidence of some raised heads in the corner the card school had begun to take an interest in the conversation.

"So you wouldn't call yourself a pacifist then?" one of them said, a massive cockney called Morley.

"Certainly not," replied Grayson in his quiet, firm manner. "Mind you, I respect a true pacifist, but I don't feel that a man should be specially favoured just because he happens to be a servant of God."

3

"How do you find our Northern hospitality then, cock?" queried Cragg.

With a smile in his voice Grayson replied, "Like you I found my way around here easily enough, even though I come from the Midlands. The only difference is I have found hospitality in the Chapel, and not in the pub. It only took me to go there one Sunday, when after the service I was surrounded by people wanting to offer hospitality. If you don't believe me ask Thorpe, or Henshaw in the next hut; or half a dozen others I could name."

A cheer, partly half-hearted and partly real, went up from the men in the hut.

When it had subsided a cockney called Oatley said, "Sure that's all very fine for you good boys, but what about us atheists, we wouldn't get much of a welcome?"

"Right on." chuckled Hilton, "we'd be too wicked for 'em, even old Cragg would be taboo in that company."

This caustic comment seemed to signal the natural end to what had already become an unsatisfactory conversation. The matter undoubtedly would have ended there had it not been for the bulky Morley abandoning the card school and lumbering into the centre of the room wearing a look of determination on his face sufficient to quell all but the most ferocious argument.

"Scoff if you like," he began on the defensive, "for I certainly make no claims to being good. I admit I like my pint with the rest, and don't bother too much about Church — but I must be fair and admit that I owe a lot to religious people. I've only got to recall Louvain in 1940, before we started the long haul back to Dunkirk. We were getting shelled to smithereens at Company Headquarters; our forward platoons had started to retreat, and when we heard this someone groaned, 'It's all up with us now; we'll never get out'."

As he spoke Morley displayed more emotion than his colleagues would ever have guessed lay behind that massive frame. He continued, "An N.C.O. heard him and snapped, 'So long as

there's a God on the Throne, Right must win..."
"I never forgot those words, and as you all know we did get out. I owe a lot to that N.C.O. and those words of encouragement. It's times like that, when your guts have turned to jelly, that you need to be reminded that Divine help is at hand; I don't care what anyone says."

To ease his emotions he pulled hard on his pipe, and with a friendly nod towards Grayson, prepared to move back to his own hut.

As he passed Oatley, the latter muttered, "Seeing is believing, all I want is for the whole thing to be over. If right wins then I'll give you and Grayson the credit."

Just at that moment the sergeant-in-waiting showed at the doorway and ordered the hut to stand to their beds. As they were all present he moved on.

The last post sounded and the hut prepared for sleep.

Rattray and Phelps lovingly steered the dolls' house into a safe haven in one corner.

Once the hut had quietened Cragg said, "I must admit I've enjoyed this evening despite the fact that it started off with an argument about Northern hospitality, floundered on about motives for joining up, and finished with a prophecy which tickled my fancy. I'll be interested to see how it all turns out."

"You ain't the only one." several voices chorused.

A yell from the sergeant-in-waiting in the direction of the hut put an end to any further attempt at conversation.

Each man was left with his own thoughts.

5

Chapter Two

A short distance outside the village where the camp was situated stood a farmhouse called Holly Farm.

It was pleasantly situated surrounded by green fields, and set back some two hundred yards from the road.

The house was occupied by a rotund elderly lady known in the vicinity as Aunt Elizabeth. She was a jolly outgoing type who, despite her seventy five years, was still rosy cheeked and full of fun.

She was known as a local 'character', and had an intimate knowledge of the 'goings on' in the district.

The troops all knew her, and as they swung past her gate on their weekly route-marches the old lady was as often as not to be seen standing waving her handkerchief, and shouting words of encouragement.

It appeared that she had assumed the role of keeping up the soldiers' morale, and during the long distressing years of the Second World War many soldiers passed her gate.

In the event she regarded them all as 'her boys', and each and every one was known to her and precious in her sight.

Half way between the village and Holly Farm the road ran over the brow of a steep hill. At the top stood an old seat extensively carved with the names and initials of some of the weary travellers who had used it over the years.

Naturally this seat was taboo to soldiers on a route march, for inevitably they were forced to breast the hill at a fast pace as a test of fitness. As a result, by the time they reached the seat panting and sweating, many envious eyes were cast in its direction.

However, during the precious off-duty times the seat was the recipient of many a service buttocks.

Normally Saturday and Sunday afternoons were off-duty periods for the unit unless of course a soldier happened to be on guard or on punishment, or an exercise had been laid on requiring the participation of all ranks. Apart from these restrictions everyone was free to 'walk out'.

Over the years a tradition had been built up in the unit regarding these half-days...'in bed, or out of barracks,' was a phrase which enabled a measure of quietness to be preserved for those remaining and endeavouring to catch up on loss of sleep.

On the Sunday following Morley's prophecy Cragg happened to be detailed as driver of a recreation truck. Hilton, through his usual bad luck, had been detailed for guard. While he stood on sentry at the front of his box in the cold November air, saluting passing officers and looking very sorry for himself, he was forced to watch the truck fill with his smiling off-duty mates.

"All aboard the Skylark." shouted Cragg, as he rammed home the tailboard. He jumped into the driving seat, started the engine, grinned evilly at Hilton, and muttered "You lucky beggar."

In a cloud of dust the truck ground out of the barrack area leaving Hilton to brood on what he was missing.

Inside the hut, Phelps and Rattray, true to form for those remaining in, left the dolls' house in its corner, assumed the horizontal position on their palliasses, and watched Grayson, in his best battledress, depart for afternoon Chapel.

The latter looked in at Thorpe's hut on the way and collected his friend.

The two walked briskly out of Camp, Grayson taking time to wink at Hilton 'on stag' as he passed him. They moved briskly up the road to the village and Chapel.

They were early, but were soon joined by Peter Cunningham. A short while later Henshaw entered and took up his position at the organ.

The whole atmosphere inside the little Chapel was so homely that each of the friends found little difficulty in letting his thoughts wander homewards to his own Home-Chapel.

The preacher was an elderly layman who had cycled several miles just to take the service. At its conclusion he shook hands with each of them.

As before, invitations were heaped upon them, and soon the four friends found themselves in the home of a Mr Edgar Fenton.

The family were quiet, God-fearing folk, who in spite of war-time austerity, always managed to make their rations stretch to cope with their guests.

The friends relaxed in the comforting glow of the sitting-room fire, and before long they were joined by Mr Fenton's daughter Clare and several of her friends. Soon the room was filled with spontaneous laughter.

The old preacher had also been invited for tea, as he required some sustenance to give him the strength to cycle further into the country to take an evening service.

In a broad Yorkshire accent Mr Fenton asked Thorpe where he came from.

"Melton Mowbray," was the answer.

"Ah thought it were somewhere special; you seem different from your mates and us ordinary folk." said his host.

Thorpe smiled self-consciously. The truth of the matter was he was different. He was twenty four, and came from a family of some repute in his town. He had a Batchelor of Arts degree from Cambridge, and though a smaller build than his comrades, his intense face, figure, and his manners all bore the hallmark of good breeding. In essence he was more of a scholar than a soldier.

Mr Fenton probed the same question at the others. In turn they replied...Philip Henshaw from Blackpool, Peter Cunningham from Newcastle, and Don Grayson from Birmingham.

Their host mentioned that war tends to throw people together from all parts of the country. He told them he'd served in the last war, in the East Yorkshire Regiment. He remarked on the size of the friends, stating that he'd never seen so many tall soldiers gathered together in one place before.

The preacher confirmed this, and said that at morning service he'd seen a soldier so tall that

8

he really thought his head would touch the roof.

"That'll be Percy Weatherall," said Thorpe. "He's big all right, he's not in our company, but he's a friend."

"What height is he?" asked the preacher.

"Nearly six feet eight inches." said Thorpe.

Silence greeted this, and Thorpe was inwardly amused to see his audience attempting the necessary mental adjustment at the thought of such manhood.

"Well, we've quite a few in our company six feet five and over, and built in proportion. We'll need 'em all, for in war brawn baffles brains." Cunningham laughed.

This drew the ladies into the conversation, so much so that they all began talking at once. Finally through the noise Mr Fenton attracted Clare's attention and asked her to set the table. She did so, assisted by a pretty black-eyed, dark haired girl called Lorna.

While they waited to eat, their host turned to Henshaw and asked him to play a tune at the small organ tucked away in a corner of the room.

He did so, and with considerable gusto they all sang, choosing their favourite songs in turn. Finally, with little effort, they did justice to the tea-table.

Afterwards, Mrs Fenton suggested that later the girls might like to take their friends to see Aunt Elizabeth.

Eventually they all arrived at Holly Farm where they were officially introduced to Aunt Elizabeth and her daughter Amy. Here they again stuffed themselves with fruit and cream cakes, which rounded off a very pleasant evening. They left Holly Farm with an open invitation to return any time.

Outside it was dark, and the road was covered with a generous layer of ice. Finally, after much giggling and holding of hands, the eight surmounted the hill and collapsed onto the long-suffering seat.

Eventually ingrained military discipline prevailed, and the four soldiers reluctantly returned to camp after saying good-bye to their pretty escorts.

9

Hilton was in the guardroom when they got back.

"Well, had a good time?" he snapped, stamping his feet vigorously to assist the circulation.

"Fantastic." they said in unison.

"Some people have all the luck." grumbled Hilton, blowing a nose which was quite purple with the cold.

Chapter Three

Next morning the main part of the company fell in for drill parade, with the exception of several drivers from the Transport Platoon, in which for once Hilton was lucky enough to be included, and the senior soldier from each hut. These latter were detailed to present their respective huts in good order for the morning's room inspection.

Phelps was detailed to represent his hut. He set about the job with little enthusiasm, muttering such words of comfort to himself as he could muster. He was about half-way through when the inspecting officer appeared in the doorway, followed at a respectful distance by several N.C.O's.

Instinctively Phelps sprang to attention, saluted smartly, and said "Hut ready for inspection, sir."

He remained perfectly motionless, his morale at zero, forlornly hoping that the officer might think things were not as bad as they looked.

Undeterred, the officer inspected each kit meticulously, and the note-taking N.C.O. at his side seemed to get busier and busier.

Inwardly quaking, Phelps began to fear that the hut would 'go up in bad order' when suddenly his luck changed.

The officer's eye fell on the dolls' house, partially covered by a ground-sheet, tucked away in a corner.

"What's that?" he rasped.

"A--a dolls house, sir."

"A dolls' house, what's it doing here?"

"It's for Rattray's little girl, sir. We're making it for Christmas," stammered Phelps.

"Good heavens; who's making it for her?" queried the surprised officer.

"I am, for one, sir," Phelps relaxed a fraction.

"Well, well, well." exclaimed the officer in genuine admiration. "When do you work on it?"

"In the evening, sir, after duty," explained Phelps.

Miraculously the officer's interest had been transferred from the state of the hut to the doll's house.

"How really splendid, Phelps. Would you ever make one for my little girl? I'll pay you for it."

The transformation from the feeling of martyrdom to one of mild approbation now complete, Phelps took the initiative.

"I dare say we could, sir," he volunteered cautiously, "though it's a bit close to Christmas to have it finished by then."

"Never mind about Christmas, the New Year'll do. One cannot get dolls' houses these days for love nor money. I'd forfeit a months' pay to get my hands on a good one. This rotten war, how it's messed up our children's lives..."

This about turn finally altered the course of the inspection in Phelps, favour, and with an old soldier's instinct he took full advantage of it.

"We'll start on it as soon as we've finished this one, sir," he promised. His confidence had returned like circulation in a hot bath.

"But," he added slyly, "the speed of production will depend on how much off-duty I get, sir."

"Very well then," said the officer, not rising to the bait but preparing to move to the next hut, "I'll take you at your word, Phelps."

With that, and not before he'd cancelled the list of the hut's defects, he disappeared with his covey of N.C.O's in attendance, leaving Phelps to thank his lucky stars that the model, whose materials had not cost him a single penny - being all looted, purloined or donated - had saved not only the name of the hut, but his skin in particular.

At ten o'clock the Battalion was allowed half an hour's break to visit the canteen. Here men fortified themselves with tea and 'wads', the latter expression covering the whole range of cakes and pastries to be had in the canteen.

'Wads' had their rivals, for in the main street of the village were two cafes, one at either end, where the home-made scones and cakes created a very real competition. It was therefore no great surprise that many soldiers found their way to one or other of these cafes in preference to the canteen.

Here, for half an hour, the noise was

indescribable when the conversation consisted of the daily ration of threats, jokes, and general rumour-spreading about the state of the war.

After his narrow escape with the inspecting officer, Phelps waited impatiently for break-time to join the gathering at the top-end cafe.

Once there he regaled a group in a corner with a full account of how the dolls' house had saved the day; at the same time he proudly disclosed his contract for yet another model.

This amused everyone except Morley, who had been put 'in report' as being the representative for his hut, which had been declared to be in very bad order.

Instead of joining in the fun Morley was unable to resist the temptation to accuse Phelps of 'crawling' to a superior officer to avoid sharing the same fate.

Just then someone said that they had heard on good authority that the whole battalion was to be granted a month's leave for Christmas. This set the place in an uproar, everyone expressing his opinion of what substance there might be in this particular rumour.

"Go on with you, that's a typical cookhouse rumour," Morley bawled above the din.

By this stage of the war it had become a well known fact that most of the more interesting rumours had their origin in the cookhouse, where the incentive was for tongues to wag even harder than in the cafes. Anyhow no rumour, however outrageous was ever allowed for long to interfere with th e steady flow of tea and scones which was the lifeblood of cafe life. Finally Morley recovered enough of his equanimity to polish off a large plate of scones and several cups of tea.

After duties that day Phelps and Rattray went straight to work on the dolls' house, and by lights out they had the structure completely finished.

Next evening they pasted the whole thing over with a paper-pattern which they had obtained from some secret source. At the conclusion it was an expert piece of craftmanship, with its red-tiled roof, latticed windows, brick-coloured door, and cream walls.

Rattray surveyed it with ill-concealed admiration. "Just in time Phelps old lad; just in time. I'm on weekend leave this Saturday, so I'll take it home with me. It's my only chance before Christmas."

The news that the dolls' house was finally completed spread like wildfire through the company, with many men coming in to view it during the course of the evening. This resulted in the two mates receiving a steady stream of congratulations.

"How on earth are you going to get it home, Rattray?" someone asked.

"By the 'Flyer' of course," said Rattray confidently.

"It'll be some job, especially with all the blokes who catch the Flyer on Saturday morning for leave," someone else said.

'The Flyer' was one of the trains which ran daily between York and the outlying districts – one trip down in the morning, and one up in the evening. Its speed bore a direct relationship to its age, for it was one of the smallest and oldest engines still in commission, and owing to the war, had never been replaced. The sum total of its carriages consisted of two plus a guard's van.

Despite these handicaps it did yeoman service at a time of national emergency, especially on leave-mornings, when it would puff into a station, smothered in a cloud of steam which oozed out of its many leaky parts; finally sniffing and snorting, like some drunken mule, to a halt.

Soon its carriages would be crammed to the roof with between two and three hundred khaki-clad figures, to say nothing of the civilian passengers.

The remark caused Rattray to think; but just then both Cragg and Grayson announced that they were due for weekend leave too, and they would gladly give a hand to get the dolls' house onto the Flyer.

Phelps felt that they would do well to take every precaution against damage that they could at this stage. He suggested that they construct a light wooden frame for the dolls' house to travel

14

in. Once inside the frame it could be well packed with paper, and sewn up in sacking, with two loops stitched to the outside to carry it by.

Accordingly they devoted another evening to making the frame, and when this was done there was a frantic search in kit-bags and under palliasses for sufficient paper and sacking to satisfy Phelps' requirements.

The protective frame greatly increased the size and weight of the dolls' house, to such an extent that Cragg and Grayson seriously began to doubt the wisdom of their decision to assist their mate on his homeward journey.

Eventually Saturday morning arrived. Long before the first notes of reveille had sounded the leave party was on its way, each man immaculate in his best uniform, with brasses highly polished.

Rattray and Grayson led the way carrying the crated dolls' house between them, with Cragg bringing up the rear, ready to catch the precious burden if any mishap should occur on the slippery road.

Every few hundred yards along the mile and a half walk to the station they halted and rested. Here the man behind would change places with one of those in front. With the dual hazard of the ice-covered road surface and the quite considerable weight of the dolls' house, it was nothing short of a miracle that they reached the station on time.

Had it been an Army task they were carrying out, they would have been complaining the whole way; but seeing it was for a domestic matter, and for one of their number, no one so much as squeaked.

Needless to say they were relieved when they reached the station, and even more relieved when "the Flyer", crammed to the roof, rattled alongside the platform. As the two carriages were jammed to capacity the three were forced to seek refuge in the guards van, which was quickly becoming choc-a-bloc too.

"No more, no more; you can't bring that parcel in here." was the cry from inside.

With a superhuman effort Grayson wriggled and

squirmed his way in. Then somehow Cragg followed suit. The train was about to start and Rattray was still on the platform clutching the dolls' house, when the two already inside, forseeing the danger, pushed and fought till they could turn around to face Rattray. Then leaning against the mass of humanity already in the carriage, they bent down and grabbed Rattray by the scruff of the neck and under each arm. Working together they somehow managed to haul him up.

All this time Rattray had held grimly onto the dolls' house, being forced to use both hands. As a result he was still suspended in the doorway as the train started to move.

By now the tenacity of the three mates had aroused a ready response from inside the carriage, and soon half a dozen willing pairs of hands dragged Rattray into the safety of the carriage just as the guard slid the door closed.

"What've you got there?" asked one of the men who'd helped Rattray in.

"A dolls' house."

"What—ho." laughed the soldier, "so you've been working hard too?"

He held up a small scooter which he was taking home, and from the grinning faces inside the carriage it was obvious that many others had similar articles with them. All were agreed however that Rattray's effort was nothing short of heroism.

The Flyer responded magnificently to the occasion, and although the extra weight of men and parcels added considerably to its load, it soon gathered momentum and careered along at its normal twenty five m.p.h.

Within the hour the three friends were unloading the dolls' house onto York station. There Cragg and Grayson took their farewell and wished Rattray luck in getting his cargo back to his home in Hull.

When they saw Rattray again after the leave was over the first question they asked was "How did you get on?"

"First class; even the conductress helped me off with it at my own door." he said.

16

Chapter Four

The Sunday following his weekend leave Grayson found himself on guard. That same week Cunningham had been hospitalised in York with what turned out to be a troublesome knee injury, which kept him out of action for several months. Henshaw was on leave, so Thorpe was the only member of the party at Chapel that day, apart from a soldier called Sawyer, who was a shy man, and kept apart from his fellows.

Thorpe therefore had the field to himself, so he gratefully accepted the invitation of a Mr and Mrs Hewlett to spend the afternoon with them and their daughter Ruth.

Knowing how much all the lads must have been missing home life, the Hewletts kindly issued an 'open house' invitation to Thorpe or any of his mates at any time.

The Sunday before Christmas Henshaw was doing his turn at guard, so Thorpe and Grayson needed little pressing to join the Hewlett family and some of their relations for tea. They quickly formed a male gathering around the fire, while the ladies busied themselves preparing a meal in the dining-room.

After helping to move several large armchairs, the friends were about to return to their seats, when they saw silhouetted in the doorway the loveliest young woman they'd ever seen. Not tall, she had light chestnut hair, and a pair of strikingly beautiful blue eyes set in an aristocratic face. Her figure was superb, and her whole bearing gave the impression of breeding.

The two men were quite stunned at the sight of her, and must have conveyed the impression that they had seen a ghost. Neither made any attempt to move, but remained rooted to the spot, their expression displaying a mixture of admiration and awe.

Fortunately, at that moment Mrs Hewlett appeared and was quick to notice the embarrassment of the three young people.

"Have you met my niece?"

"No." they answered together.

17

"Hilary, this is Mr Thorpe, and Mr Grayson."

They shook hands self-consciously, then stood dumbly waiting for something to happen.

Grayson noticed that his young comrade had more colour than usual, and that every time Hilary's eyes met his they would drop and his cheeks would assume a deeper tinge.

Finally, to break the stalemate, Hilary suggested that they all sit down, which they agreed to readily enough, feeling it more expedient to stay where they were rather than risk returning to the drawing room. Thorpe battled to overcome his shyness, and partly succeeded. Finally he said, "We'd no idea that Mrs Hewlett had a niece living here."

"Didn't you?" smiled Hilary, her expressive blue eyes indicating that she was enjoying the little joke at their expense. "Actually I don't live here, I'm just spending Christmas."

This begged the next question from Thorpe, which wasn't long in coming.

"Where do you come from?" Thorpe's curiosity was now thoroughly aroused.

"I live in Leeds," she said in her well modulated, refined voice. "Father has a warehouse there."

"Is that so? You'll be glad to have a spell away from the business world then," Thorpe said.

"Yes indeed, though actually I don't come in contact much with it, my work is teaching pianoforte," she said.

"Now that is interesting," said Thorpe, his voice rising with excitement. He was an accomplished pianist, and passionately fond of music. "That's something I've always wanted to do, to teach music."

Suitably encouraged, they both embarked upon a discussion about music, and their favourite composers.

Eventually they were interrupted by Mrs Hewlett announcing that tea was ready.

Although the tea-table, as usual, was full to overflowing with good things, Thorpe had his eyes firmly fixed on Hilary and devoted most of his time to conversation with her. Indeed he appeared reluctant to lose her interest for more than a second at a time.

After the meal they all adjourned to the drawing-room where Thorpe prevailed upon the girl to play a selection of tunes on the piano. These she executed with such aplomb that his opinion of her rose even higher.

Later, on the way back to camp, it didn't require a genius to interpret the reason for Thorpe's terse replies to his friend's questions.

Undoubtedly he had fallen head-over-heels in love with Hilary.

From then onwards Thorpe took every opportunity to visit the Hewlett household, and Hilary in particular.

Sometime later he rounded on Grayson, displeased with the latter's reaction to his courtship. Grayson had told him bluntly, "Such luxuries as Miss Hilary aren't for the likes of you and me."

After some verbal 'fisticuffs' on this subject, it turned out that Grayson, who totally approved of Hilary as a person, was only trying to give his friend good advice, pointing out that in wartime one had to be ultra careful where friendships with the opposite sex were concerned. He further went on to point out that Thorpe, as an ordinary soldier, would find himself in considerable difficulties if he allowed the relationship to go any further. If he'd taken a commission things might have been different, but in the circumstances, as he'd chosen to serve in the rank and file, this in itself should limit his intentions towards Hilary.

Thorpe remained silent during all the time, turning over in his mind the obvious painful truth of his friend's words. He was not a stupid man, and he realised that he had come to a cross-roads in his life.

Although he obviously held all the qualities necessary for a commission he had purposely avoided taking one. Now the situation had changed, and for the first time in his career he felt at a loss.

"Perhaps she'll wait for me till this is all

over," he said with a confidence he didn't feel.

"Anybody's guess," Grayson shrugged. "Don't forget thousands of women are in the same boat. War is a false state, you know. Don't forget also that the Hewletts and Fentons, and doubtless many others, out of sheer kindness, are opening their houses to us, and we have a duty in turn to show our appreciation by not getting involved with their families. I'm sure the girls have only one thought, and that's to be sociable to us in our time of need."

Thorpe wasn't too sure about that, but he did agree to go cautiously in the matter of Hilary.

Chapter Five

As it was by now fast approaching the festive season word got around that the local 'Chapel-folk' would be glad of assistance from the men in camp to make up carol singing parties. The Hewlett party was scheduled to go out on Christmas Eve, and the Fentons' on Christmas Day.

As Henshaw had been the spokesman in this matter, and had taken the liberty of offering all their services to both parties, Thorpe and Grayson were, to say the least, dismayed. Especially the latter, who had a very limited capacity for singing of any sort. Needless to say there were the usual cracks passed amongst the hut members.

"Can't fail to make your name; people'll think you are the town crier," scoffed Hilton at Grayson's expense. "As for Thorpe, he'll do an excellent imitation of a fog-horn."

True to Army form, on the run-up to Christmas all training virtually ground to a halt, and only a minimum of duties, just enough to maintain control, were ordered through the companies.

The latest camp rumour circulating at the time was news of a massive exercise due to be launched in the Yorkshire countryside early in the New Year. This indicated to all but the least intelligent that the long-promised second front couldn't be far off, and that the exercise was merely to be the touch-paper for the big push.

Accordingly, everyone was in agreement that Christmas 1943 must be the best Christmas they'd ever had...

To add a touch of real Yuletide character to the proceedings, the weather suddenly took a turn for the worse, until the whole countryside from the Pennines to the North Sea was blanketed in thick choking fog.

Not even this could dampen the spirits of the men, and it wasn't long before recreation trucks were leaving the camp in all directions, like ants deserting an anthill.

The carollers, Thorpe, Henshaw and Grayson,

moved out of the camp en route for the village just at the same time as the recreation men were piling into trucks. Judging by the noise it seemed that most of the company were headed for York.

"Up the carol-singers." roared a voice from the back of a truck. "You'd better block your ears up and grab each other on the top notes, in case you don't get down."

The chums took the ribbing in good part and made their way to the Hewletts', where Henshaw and Grayson went to the Chapel to collect a small portable organ. Thorpe, not surprisingly, helped Hilary to clean and fill the lanterns. He must have done well at this, for when the others returned the two were on Christian name terms. Realising the disadvantage of this so far as the others were concerned, Ruth suggested that from now on they all call each other by their Christian names.

Promptly by nine o'clock the dozen or so carollers had assembled at the house. Mr Hewlett took charge and led the party into the street. At the head of the group strode Thorpe carrying a lantern, while Henshaw and Grayson brought up the rear with the organ.

They moved cautiously to the end of the village, endeavouring to keep their balance on the slippery road. Here they halted in a gateway, positioned their lanterns, grouped around the organ, and despite the intense cold, soon warmed to their task.

The rise and fall of their voices coming out of the fog, and the light from the lanterns accentuating the contrast of their white faces and darks forms, gave them a ghostly appearance.

They sang a number of 'old faithfuls' and before long the three had lost all vestiges of stage fright and were singing as lustily as the rest. Henshaw sang tenor, and Grayson attempted bass, while Thorpe was not too sure what he sang. In any event he was much preoccupied with Hilary, who stood opposite him. In her white hooded coat and with the light of the lantern shining full upon her, she looked positively angelic. She saw him watching her, and returned his interest with a smile which lit up her whole face, and which by now he knew tc be an important part of her charm.

Finally the evening drew to a close and the three returned to camp, well pleased with their carolling efforts.

Next morning there was a small bonus in the shape of reveille being half an hour later than normal. The Army, not being an organisation renowned for handing out bonuses as a matter of course, did do its best to make things easier for its servants on Christmas Day. Breakfast extras also appeared in the shape of fried eggs and coffee.

Most of the morning was spent doing not a lot in the huts. Naturally each man's thoughts turned to his loved ones at home – in particular Rattray pondered, with some emotion, on the vision of his children's faces when they opened the doll's house.

Shortly after midday, the whole company attired in best battledress, sat down to do justice to their Christmas dinner. As was the custom, on the arrival of the officers the toasting ceremony was performed, followed by resounding cheers for the Quartermaster and Quartermaster sergeant for their efforts in producing the spread. Afterwards, replete with Christmas fare, the bulk of the company piled onto the recreation transport and set off to enjoy the remainder of their day.

The friends gathered to form another carol-party, this time at the Fentons. Afterwards they gathered for refreshments. The cold had been intense, but Mrs Fenton soon made short work of that by providing plentiful supplies of cocoa.

The day was rounded off nicely by a visit to Aunt Elizabeth.... Holy Farm looked a treat, and as its name implied, the inside was liberally strewn with holly. Aunt Elizabeth apologised for not having any mistletoe, for if there had been any she would have dragged each of the boys under it in turn and kissed them, she said. No one really doubted that the same formidable lady would have fulfilled her threat, but under the circumstances they said they would take the will for the deed.

All good things must come to an end, and eventually the friends found their way back to camp, their pockets bulging with Aunt Elizabeth's mince-pies.

Thorpe fell asleep, his mind crammed with thoughts for Hilary, and what her feelings might be towards him. In the circumstances he was unable to plan for the future, but all in all he didn't feel too displeased with the present.

Next evening, under the pretext of using the Hewlett's telephone for a long-distance call, Thorpe called to see Hilary. Whilst there he received an invitation for himself and his friends to a party at the Hewlett home the following eveing. It turned out to be quite a happy family gathering, complete with Christmas tree and games; the last of the festive season's celebrations, bringing to a close a happy time for the friends.

It didn't go unnoticed by Thorpe that for the most of the evening Grayson and Mr. Hewlett had sat in a corner with their heads together, both looking ominously serious. Indeed Grayson continued to wear the same expression long after he had returned to camp.

Next day, when Grayson's attitude towards Thorpe continued to be remote, the latter finally suspected that something was indeed wrong. He picked a suitable time to accompany Grayson to the reading room. Here he tackled him.

"Quiet? what do you mean?" rasped Grayson, immediately on the defensive.

"You know very well what I mean," said Thorpe firmly.

Momentarily silent, Grayson finally made up his mind.

"Well Arthur, there's something which I know, and if you were told, would hurt you very much. Obviously, as you are my friend I'm reluctant to tell you."

"Come on, out with it, that's what friends are for," Thorpe said, his eyes staring.

Another long pause, then, obviously uncomfortable, Grayson finally said, "All right

Arthur, if that's what you want. In fact if you recollect our previous conversation you probably already know what it's about."

"Hilary, I suppose?" said Thorpe with ill-concealed patience.

Grayson nodded.

"Well let's have it." Thorpe exploded.

"You must have noticed that Mr Hewlett and I were deep in conversation last night?" Grayson said, speaking deliberately.

Thorpe nodded, waiting.

"He made it quite clear that he didn't wish to be thought intruding..." Grayson finally warmed to his theme. "At the same time he wished to point out that all the warmth and kindness which the young ladies - including Hilary - showed us, was purely of a sociable nature in an attempt to make our stay in the area as pleasant as possible, and nothing deeper than that should be read into their attitudes.

"I see," said Thorpe after a long pause, his face colouring.

"Hilary's parents would not wish her to develop an emotional attachment at this time to you or anybody else, and Mr Hewlett feels obliged to protect her interests so long as she is in his house."

"I see," said Thorpe again. This time his face was white.

"He was not resentful about it in any way, quite the reverse, he genuinely liked having us all about the house, but merely felt in everyone's interests the matter should be mentioned."

"I see," said Thorpe a third time. "So that's it then?"

"'Fraid so Arthur, and I really wish it wasn't," Grayson sighed.

"Oh well, it's just a cross I'll have to bear," said Thorpe, trying to keep his voice steady. "They say time's a great healer."

"You really mustn't think there's anything personal in it old lad," Grayson said comfortingly. "And you must know that Mr Hewlett has the highest regard for you, but......" he spread his hands, "it's just the way things are."

"I can see that," Thorpe sighed heavily. "There are really only two consolations in the matter; one, that I didn't know the true situation before Christmas, otherwise it would have spoiled it; and the other is that I have you as a friend. I promise I'll not show my true feelings towards Hilary any more; it'll be hard going, but with God's help I'll do it."

Grayson stood up and gripped his friend by the shoulder. "You'll do it, and you'll prove yourself a man in the process. Something else'll turn up, you'll see."

"I expect you're right, Don; you usually are." Thorpe managed a half-hearted grin, and sloped off to his hut which he was glad to find empty.

Of all the times in his entire career this was one in which he needed to be alone. He needed to think and plan; he needed to learn how to re-adjust his thoughts towards Hilary, to show a friendly and caring face, but nothing more...

Chapter Six

About this time a strange quirk of fate overtook the friends. For several days each had been complaining of a sore throat, but none attached great significance to this till the day after Grayson's disclosure to Thorpe.

By then each was so badly affected that they could hardly talk. They put this down to their concerted efforts at carolling, but despite the hoarseness of their voices, they remained on duty.

The matter finally came to an unpleasant head when Henshaw, the only one of the party who'd been to the Fentons', informed them that Clare had developed measles on Boxing Day, and had been removed to York. It didn't take long for the connection to be obvious, so the friends reported sick. An examination revealed no special symptoms, so they were ordered to gargle and report to the medical officer twice daily till further notice.

They spent an anxious few days in this manner, and were vastly relieved when their throats finally cleared up with not further ill-effects. This confirmed the original theory that the prolonged bout of carol singing had been the root cause all the time.

As a result of all this it was several days before they were able once again to visit the Hewletts. This time Thorpe, true to his word, confronted Hilary with a singular reserve, which did not go unnoticed.

Indeed it became obvious that Hilary was moved at his 'climb down' in tempo. It was the eve of her return to Leeds, and she approached Thorpe with a certain amount of nervousness, almost as though she would have liked to have said something, but found herself unable to.

The New Year had come in with a bang, and was not long in making its presence felt by way of a spell of freezing cold and fog. Training for the men began again in earnest, and the never-ending series of drills, exercises, guards and fatigues, became once again the order of the day. There was little time off and Phelps, who

27

had reached an all time low, felt the time had come to honour his contract with the officer to make the dolls' house; thereby hopefully to escape some unpleasant duty.

Soon his enthusiasm for the task showed no bounds, so much so that before long he had persuaded himself that this was as much a duty towards his country as were the activities of his less fortunate comrades. This spate of enthusiasm continued unabated until one day news filtered through the company office that he was due for leave. The announcement of this coincided exactly with his loss of enthusiam for the dolls' house project.

His pals were highly amused at this about-face, which, for those who knew him well, was not entirely unexpected. Forced to back-pedal, Phelps finally admitted that while the dolls' house project was still important, no way was it as important as leave. The rest of the hut agreed unanimously...

Quick to capitalise on the situation, Rattray enquired if he and Cragg could continue the project while Phelps was on leave. Realising what was at stake, Phelps declined the offer, and made some excuse about his design being different from any else's.

Consequently the dolls' house project remained in limbo for some considerable time due to the fact that towards the end of his leave Phelps cleverly managed to develop influenza. When he did finally return the one factor which had kept him from going permanently a.w.o.l. had been the thought of the dolls' house. This was short-lived however, for immediately on his return rumours emanated from the cafes to the effect that a very large exercise was planned within the next few days. This was to be the climax of all their years of training - an exercise to end all exercises. The highest standards would be demanded of men and materials. This would mean hour upon hour of work on the vehicles, linked to never-ending inspections.

Being a driver, and responsible for a three-tonner, Phelps had little time to spare for building dolls' houses. Finally the external pressures on him became so great that he ultimately abandoned the project altogether.

As the day signalling the start of the exercise drew nearer, 'the enemy' were detailed to take up positions in certain remote countryside vantage points. As all the friends had already camped and trained in the surrounding countryside, they knew all these areas like the back of their hands. At the time they had camped, the countryside had been looking its best with field upon field of waving corn, interspersed with isolated woods, and dotted with tiny pepper-pot sized villages.

Now, with the vicious arrival of the New Year, it looked bare and windswept. Each day was the subject of fresh storms of snow and sleet. One spot in particular had become ominously familiar to the friends; it consisted simply of a cross-roads, which for conveniece, had been used on most of their previous exercises as the 'objective'. Once this was reached the battle was considered to be over and won. Consequently it had become a symbol of good – a good place – in the minds of the men. A place where the backbreaking, and often frightening, exercises ground to a halt.

It was little wonder therefore that this particular cross-roads was tipped in the cafes as once more to become the key-stone for the exercise.

Strict orders were issued that no food was to be bought from either shops, or civilians, for the duration of the exercise, as this was to be a complete test of the men's ability to endure everything that was thrown at them during the exercise, sustained only by army issue food. As a counter measure vast quantities of scones and cakes were consumed in the cafes in the few days running up to the start of the exercise.

In next to no time they were all in the thick of it. Cragg and Phelps were detailed to drive three tonners, Hilton a 15 cwt Bedford, Rattray one of the officers' cars; whilst Oatley and Grayson were tasked as relief drivers – Grayson, largely because he was shortly to go on leave –

an unbelievable stroke of good fortune.

The column wound through lanes and into villages. It wasn't long before the third class roads which they had to use were reduced to quagmires from the weight of the long line of tanks and trucks, many of which became bogged down awaiting the arrival of recovery vehicles. Every now and again an armoured car would waltz gracefully across the road in a never ending slide, only to finish up in the ditch as the soft ground gave way under its weight.

The tractor-drivers, towing the anti-tank guns, had a particularly unpleasant time, with their charges constantly capsizing or skidding on corners, resulting in the smashing of one fence after another.

By late afternoon of the first day the battalion was half-way to the starting point of the exercise. By now it was sleeting hard and everyone was numb from head to foot.

To add to their troubles the fog started to thicken and the wind freshened. By nightfall all troops had reached their 'harbouring area', and all ranks, to a man, felt blue, looked blue, and were under no illusions that at long last they had entered 'The War Games'.

Taciturnly they took up defensive positions in the fields surrounding some farms, spread camouflage nets over their vehicles, and did their best to assemble their kit for a night's sleep – such as it would be.

In an attempt to keep the circulation going much foot-stamping went on. which if nothing else, helped to pass the time. Finally, after interminable delays, cocoa, plus the inevitable bully-beef and biscuits, was served.

"Come and get it." thundered the Quartermaster-sergeant in time-honoured fashion. The company, like so many drowning rats emerging from a sewer, did just that.

They split up into groups around their trucks, and sipped the cocoa slowly to make it spin out. At first they were too demoralised to make any attempt at conversation, but after a while, as the cocoa began to work its way down each body, spirits rose, individually at first, and then in groups where the usual 'wise-cracker' took control.

Finally the weary men, less those detailed for guard, clambered into their trucks or lay on groundsheets beside their vehicles, in a brave attempt at sleep. Soon the exposed bodies were blanketed by sleet, and the very marrow of their bones became penetrated by cold.

Next day they moved northwards, where they again harboured in some woods surrounding a small partly-frozen lake. Here they stayed for several days, still not yet 'in action'. Each day nature entertained them with its full repertoire of winter weather conditions, and in turn they endured rain, sleet, snow and wind.

Poor Thorpe was particularly unhappy. Dejectedly he stood by a truck, his rifle slung over his shoulder, and watched a jeep ploughing its way through a field of mud, skidding this way and that, mostly out of control, scattering a shower of dirt from its wheels over a group of officers who were huddled together pouring over a map.

"Cheer up mate." a voice said.

He looked up to see Henshaw grinning at him as he squelched through the mud towards his truck.

"Not possible," stammered Thorpe, his expression depicting his feelings of despair.

Realising communication was impossible, Henshaw moved on. He returned in a few minutes with his hands behind his back. Up close he whispered, "Guess what I've got?"

"Haven't a clue," Thorpe said disinterestedly.

"A letter, and from Leeds too." Henshaw revealed his right hand and shoved it into Thorpe's face.

The latter's face brightened as he made a wild grab at the letter. Successful, he examined the address and post-mark. Suddenly a sheer spasm of joy shot through him. He looked up and saw Henshaw's smiling face.

"Hilary?"

He tore open the envelope. his eyes devouring

31

the contents. Henshaw waited patiently, aware of the latter's tension.

"She says Ruth wrote and mentioned we were on this exercise, and she couldn't sleep thinking about us stuck up here in all this mud and arctic weather. So she just had to drop us a line to let us know we were all in her thoughts – what do you think of that?" Thorpe blurted out.

"She's a grand girl, there's no doubt of it," Henshaw agreed.

In his excitement Thorpe began to pace up and down. He became completely oblivious to his surroundings, for his mind was working overtime, imagining himself back at the Hewletts'.

Through his haze of happiness one thought stuck in his mind, and that was that Hilary must still have some regard for him otherwise she wouldn't have bothered to write. He was thinking out a suitable reply when suddenly the cold hand of depression squeezed at his heart – his promise to show her no more special attention. For five minutes there ensued an internal struggle as strong as anything he'd ever experienced, which finally resolved itself in his better-self prevailing.

Seizing upon the only possible consolation, he said with unusual courage, "Oh well, she did ask for all of us."

Notwithstanding the affirmation of his decision yet again, the very fact of Hilary's letter arriving gave Thorpe fresh heart to face the rigours of the exercise which he knew were inevitable. Nor did he allow himself to become depressed as he watched Grayson set off on leave...

The exercise swung into being remorselessly. By the fifth day all units had moved forward a little. This process was repeated each ensuing day.

For miles around the roads and fields were positively choked with men and vehicles, and the quagmire they created made it well nigh impossible to distinguish where the fields ended and the roads began. Snow and sleet paid their daily visit, and the constant stream of 'bully-beef' and biscuits was the only fare the soldiers knew. By the tenth day the forward units had reached the finishing point, which in terms of true mileage was a mere twenty miles from the starting point.

Apparently the object of the exercise had been achieved to the organisers' satisfaction, so the order was given to disperse.

Back at camp Thorpe went on what he considered to be some well-earned leave.

Chapter Seven

On his return from leave in early March Thorpe received the unpleasant news that he had been posted to Divisional Headquarters. This of course meant separation from his friends – something which hardly bore thinking about. To make matters worse he had to move within two days.

Stoically he bore this news, as he had the news of Hilary; and outwardly at least he put a good face on things. Patiently he waited till after duties that evening to inform the Chapel–folk of his fate. To soothe the blow he explained that 'Div' was not that far away, and that he would still be able to keep in touch.

Shortly after Thorpe's departure an ominous order came through to the effect that all further leave was cancelled. This was quickly followed by the censorship of all outgoing letters from the battalion, coupled with strict instructions not to fraternise with the civilian population. Recreation trucks to York were still allowed to run, but on a limited basis, and all the signs of a large move were in evidence.

Seizing their opportunity while there was still time, Henshaw and Grayson decided to have a final get–together with the girls. This included Thorpe, who happened to put in an appearance a few days later.

Duly informed, Ruth and Hilary became as enthusiastic for a meeting as the men, and a date was set for the following Saturday week – the meeting place to be the bus stop in St. Leonard's place near the Bootham Bar.

The appointed time arrived and the two parties were delighted to see each other. They lost no time in mingling with the animated crowds wending their way through York's narrow streets. It was a beautiful spring afternoon and the ancient city looked its best.

In those days York was a focal–point for the many units stationed in the surrounding area to converge there on Saturday afternoons – for them all roads led to York. In many ways York must have seemed to be in its prime during those war-time days - for not even from its earliest beginnings as a Roman fortress had it presented such a moving sight or shown such a cosmopolitan character, with its spacious market-place, wonderfully constructed historic buildings, and twisting narrow alleys compacted inside its solid stone walls. The whole was dominated by the stately old Minster.

Within these confines, on Saturday afternoons, collected a goodly cross-section of the services when soldiers, airmen, W.A.A.F's, A.T.C., Women's Land Army girls, all intermingled with the city's own denizens, who were glad to share it with these newcomers forced there by the war.

Yet despite the many thousands of service folk congregated within a comparatively small area, York always seemed capable of absorbing them all. Because of the ancient character of the place there were always fresh and interesting things to see; and the scope of its cafes, riverside, and shops, seemed to be never-ending.

Our friends were no exception to York's magic, and soon became drawn into its atmosphere. Initially they visited the Minster and walked down its beautiful spacious nave, the whole length of which breathed a message from the past which filled them with quiet awe. They moved on up the stone steps to the top of the tower, where they drank in the views over the city.

Then down Stonegate, through Daveygate, and into the Market-place, which was a constant hive of activity with servicemen strutting about in their best uniforms like so many peacocks, showing off their feathers.

Hilton and Oatley were spotted in the crowd, arm-in-arm with two pretty W.A.A.F's, their laughter carrying across the market. All the indications were that at last they had found 'Northern Hospitality' much to their liking.

The friends moved on through the Shambles, Pavement and Piccadilly, and turned into Tower St. observing Clifford's Tower, the Assize Courts, and the Old Prison as they went. Finally they crossed Skeldergate Bridge and walked along the wall towards Lendal Bridge. They were perhaps half-way across and were absorbed in the river traffic, when a stentorian bellow caused them to turn. There stood the tallest man the girls had ever seen.

There was no mistaking Percy Weatherall – once seen never forgotten. Against the setting sun he looked every inch his six feet eight inches. He approached them wearing a grin from ear to ear.

"Share the joke, Perce." said Henshaw.

In between the roars of laughter they managed to make out that Percy had just returned from a football match in which Bradford had beaten York. Being a West-Riding man born and bred this win had put the giant in a good mood, which would last at least a fortnight.

Woman-shy, Percy made heavy weather with the girls upon introduction, till Henshaw finally suggested that they move on. Falling behind the others, Percy eventually relaxed, and after a while his confidence returned, enabling him to wax eloquent over the glories of York.

The party, less Percy who, after seeing the queue outside a cafe, decided to take his chance in the Army canteen around the corner, adjourned to the cafe. Finally they managed to squeeze around a minute table, where after some indecision, Grayson ordered lamb cutlets for all – a luxury virtually unheard of in wartime.

Afterwards, as darkness had fallen, they moved up the faintly-lit streets in the blackout, bumping from time to time into many others scurrying hither and thither. Ruth led them to a hall which she knew provided light entertainment on Saturday nights. Soon they got stuck into playing darts and table-tennis.

This went on for several hours till finally Hilary reminded them that they would have to hurry to catch the night train to Leeds, which was due to leave in twenty minutes.

They declined Thorpe's offer of supper, but did succumb to 'tea and wads' which they bolted down and ran.

They made the train with seconds to spare, leaving the men to 'mark-time' till their recreation-truck turned up.

The following week preparations for a move began in earnest, and although genuine efforts were made to camouflage these activities it was impossible to operate in complete secrecy. The dismantling of apparatus, the loading and dispatch of surplus stocks of kit back to supply-dumps, tended to arouse the suspicions of the civilian population. In turn this caused the troops some embarrassment when socialising, as they had to evade questions as best they could.

Now that the evenings were drawing out once more, Cragg and Grayson had become rival gardeners. Grayson found much-needed relaxation in helping Mr Fenton in his vegetable plots, while Cragg did the same for the man next door.

Several weeks passed in this fashion, until one day, despite the fact that no specific orders had been issued to the battalion, it dawned on everyone, soldier and civilian alike, that the hour of departure, and hence the hour of separation, had come. It was an extraordinary case of inexplicable premonition, made even stranger by the fact that it was felt by all and sundry.

This coincided with the return of Peter Cunningham, their friend, from hospital, where he'd lingered for some weeks with an injured leg. He was heard to remark wryly that he knew they wouldn't let him miss the 'fun'.

Shortly after midday on Sunday all was ready for the move, when suddenly Thorpe appeared on 'the doorstep'.

"How on earth did you get here?" enquired a surprised Henshaw.

"Hitch-hiked." said Thorpe.

"So you're coming with us then?" chuckled Cunningham.

"Looks like it - that's why I came over," Thorpe said.

"Well let's make the best of the time we have left," said Cunningham with just a trace of tremor in his voice. "The only other people I'd rather be with than you blokes, are my wife and family, and as that's impossible, well..." he blew his nose - hard.

The pensive expressions on the faces of the others indicated that they were thinking something similar.

As they moved down the road to Chapel - the last time they would do so - they passed several sets of soldiers with their wives and families, who were staying in the village - all were solemn faced.

They were barely seated when the door opened and in walked Ruth and Hilary. As the girls sat down Hilary gave a quick smile in their direction. The men busied themselves wondering what could have brought her here for the week-end all the way from Leeds, and Thorpe in particular could hardly contain his curiosity till the service was over.

"I had a notion this might be your last Sunday," Hilary said when they met outside. "I felt I must come. It's good to see you again Peter - I hope you are better," she said as she shook hands with Cunningham.

He mumbled his gratitude.

"Let's all have a final tea," she said turning to Ruth. "We could if we hurry."

Ruth smiled her approval. In next to no time the friends were once again within the warmth of the Hewlett household, enjoying for the last time their hospitality.

They dreaded the farewell, which they put off as long as possible. But it had to come, and when it did Mrs Hewlett handed each a large paper bag full of 'goodies' which she'd made up for each of the friends. Tearfully she passed them over and said, "There, these will help you on your way."

Ruth and her aunt were also doing a spot of eye-wiping.

"Where's Hilary?" asked Thorpe.

No one replied, and there was silence except for a noise from the kitchen, which suddenly ceased.

"Is she in the house at all?" asked Thorpe, with a touch of panic in his voice.

Again the noise was heard...

Thorpe moved towards the kitchen door.

"Hilary, where are you?"

A crash, and the door opened. Out stepped Hilary, her sensitive face smiling a welcome, but through a veil of tears. Without hesitation she moved towards Thorpe, took his hand and quietly said, "Good-bye and God bless you."

Her hand, so small, so perfectly formed, nestled in his, like a kitten in the arms of a strong man.

"Good-bye Hilary," he stammered, stifling the urge to throw his arms around her.

She shook hands with the others, and all, without exception, looked visibly moved.

The friends started to go. Suddenly Grayson turned to the Hewletts, "Don't worry," he said with characteristic calmness, "we'll come back again some day; I've a strong conviction God'll keep us safe."

Once in the street the friends didn't dare to look back, but made for the Fenton house. Clare came out and suggested they see Aunt Elizabeth first. Within fifteen minutes they were inside Holly Farm.

The same scene which had taken place at the Hewlett's was re-enacted, and as they were leaving old Aunt Elizabeth said, "Boys, I'll pray each night for you."

At the Fenton house supper was ready, but the feelings of the lads were by now so stirred that they couldn't do justice to the meal. They sang some hymns and Mrs Fenton prayed, and poor Clare had to rush to the kitchen to hide her tears.

It was close to midnight by the time they got back to camp. Most of the company were singing or shouting – it was the last night before the move, so they were making the best of it.

None had it in them to settle, and few slept – for a change reveille was a welcome rather than unwelcome sound.

Thorpe, of course, had to return to 'Div.' As luck would have it a truck stopped and picked him up and took him all the way.

As he snuggled under his army blanket he consoled himself with the thought that she must have cared for him, for in his eyes Hilary had fought as tough as battle as he had......

Next morning the Hewletts and Fentons had recovered sufficiently to enable them to join with the rest of the village to give the troops a good send-off.

At nine o'clock the column moved slowly up the main street. Men waved and shouted their farewells to friends and relations. There was some weeping, and many handkerchiefs were in evidence, but everyone tried to be brave.

As they drove past in their trucks Henshaw, Cunningham and Grayson returned their friends' waves. The sun was shining on the white cottages, and even the cafes looked superb. The speed of the column quickened and within minutes they had passed 'the seat' which Henshaw saluted. As they reached Holly Farm old Aunt Elizabeth was at the gate, waving fit to bust.

"Good-bye Granny," was echoed from a thousand throats.

"Goodbye boys; God bless you." she kept calling.

The column built up maximum speed; its head swung around a bend in the road. Soon it was lost to view.

The villagers remained talking amongst themselves, seeking comfort in the thought that now the war would soon be over. A neighbour of Mr Fenton's remarked that in his opinion the battalion would make a name for themselves before long.

Fenton nodded solemnly several times in agreement before he disappeared into his house and closed the door.

Chapter Eight

It was 0900 on the sixth of June 1944. The South Coast Downs looked the quietest place on earth that morning, and but for a fresh sea-breeze, which rustled through the many acres of grass and stirred the scattered woods, there was nothing to mar their summer glory.

"If I hear another man say the invasion has started I'll put him on a charge. We are doing an operation behind Le Havre, as the radio said - let's have no more rumours." The company commander's voice was stern, as he moved his company onto the position he'd chosen for practising some field-firing.

The order quietened things down, but failed to control the whispering, which continued unabated. This was understandable as the men were in high spirits. Had they not heard the airborne-armada roar overhead in the early hours of the morning, as they lay in their billets? Hadn't someone heard a civilian remark that news of the Second Front had actually been broadcast?

Nothing, neither divisional commander nor company commander, could curb their excitement - that gut-feeling of speculation. To a man they were all ears, listening out for the slightest crumb of information which might fire the tinder of their curiosity.

In the event they hadn't long to wait. The field-firing had hardly commenced when up came a despatch-rider with a message for the company commander. He read it hurriedly, then turned to a subaltern and ordered him to take over. With a swift movement he hauled himself onto the motor-bike behind the despatch rider, and shot off in a cloud of dust, but not before he shouted to his second-in-command, "I'm for the advance party; see you over there."

His words settled any lingering doubts which might have remained in the minds of the men; the invasion was on - and to prove it that was the last they saw of him for three weeks.

The company continued with field-firing exercises as if nothing had happened, and returned to their billets in the afternoon.

"This is it, we'll be off to-night, mark my words." The voice was Cragg's. This was quickly answered by a chorus of wisecracks.

However no such order came that day, nor for quite a few days after, till eventually the initial enthusiasm began to wear a little thin. Since leaving Yorkshire some six weeks had already passed and many changes had taken place. Hilton, Cragg, Grayson, Oatley and Morley had all been transferred to another company, and although they saw their old acquaintances from time to time, naturally they had acquired a new set of friends – which, according to Morley, all looked fierce enough to scare the life out of any self-respecting Nazi.

Amongst a host of new names and faces were Joe Spottiswoode and Bill Crabtree, two armoured-car drivers, Tommy Calder, a jeep driver, and a couple more named Vincent and Copplestone.

Copplestone had the name of being the battalion's most expert tea-maker, and on exercises could be relied on to 'mash-down' perfectly in all weathers. Vincent was the best romancer in the company, guaranteed to garnish with lies any ordinary situation. The two drivers on the other hand boasted no particular accomplishment whatsoever, unless in the case of Calder, who admitted to being a good soldier, but only when he was in his jeep.

The coastal town where the division had 'harboured' became a hectic place in the days running up to D-day. Tanks lined streets and squares, and vehicles of all kinds roared along the sea-front. Troops were billeted in most of the houses, and filled the town with a greater noise than any peace-time holiday-making crowd could ever have done.

In the early hours of one morning they stole away – northward. Few townsfolk saw them depart, and the whole column was well clear of the town before it was realised they'd left. They took the London road and within four hours had reached the Metropolis. Inevitably their progress was slow, and became hampered by flying-bombs. But although they passed plenty of devastation en-route they themselves sustained neither damage to vehicles nor injury to men.

They crossed London Bridge, turned east, and slackening speed to a crawl, passed through Aldgate, where despite the bombs and the destruction of many of their own homes, a cheering crowd had gathered to encourage the troops on their way. It was a gallant gesture and greatly appreciated by the division.

"We didn't deserve that, you know," said Hilton, after they'd passed. "After all, they were the heroes, not us."

At this crack a certain uncomfortable redness was noted in the faces of some of the men.

Cragg said, "Yes, it took guts I wonder what it'll be like going through the streets of Berlin...if we live to see it?" To lighten the mood he added as an afterthought, "Were'nt the girls pretty?"

A lusty trooper-type roar came out of the section in answer to his remark.

No more fitting send-off could have been given, for it was entirely in tune with the mood of the men. It would inspire them in the struggle ahead of them, right to the gates of Berlin.

Within an hour they had cleared the city, eventually arriving at their destination, London Docks. Here the column was split in two, and the loading of vehicles and equipment onto two liberty ships began. This operation was completed inside twenty-four hours, and the following morning, after a short, sharp roll-call, the whole battalion embarked for Normandy.

They slept in the holds, with the minimum of space for each man. Many had to lie with their knees almost forced up to their chins. A few of the more fortunate ones acquired hammocks, which they slung above their luckless comrades.

When the ration launch unloaded its daily burden and everything was distributed, the already pint-sized sleeping spaces became even more restricted, due to the piles of bully-beef cans separating each man.

"There's enough bully here to stand a siege," growled Hilton, attempting to squeeze between rows of tins.

"Too bad, all this delay," mumbled Cragg, "but then war's ninety per cent waiting anyway." he shrugged philosophically.

Soon everyone was openly asking what the delay was all about, and as is the nature of things, many weird and wonderful opinions were expressed. Vincent produced the most frightening story of all, namely that the preceding convoy had been attacked by no less than eighty E-boats, and all the ships had been sunk.

Suddenly they moved.

From the deck of the ship Grayson stood watching the other vessel slipping out of dock and into the river, while the men of the first section of the battalion lined her rails, cat-calling to those on the other ship.

'I wonder how many of us will come back -- not too many?' Grayson mused to himself.

Once in the Thames both ships crawled slowly to the mouth of the estuary to the forming-up point for the next convoy for Normandy. Here they anchored and waited. Their convoy was expected to depart on the following day, but when it came and went without any sign of a move everyone felt despondent.

Eventually a launch drew alongside again.

"What's up now?" asked Morley, regarding it with the deepest suspicion.

"Rations probably," said Calder. "I've just heard we're here for another twenty-four hours."

Morley gave a sigh, and moved along the deck -- he just didn't want to know.

Next day the launch visited them again on the same mission. By the time the third day had come and gone the popularity of the little ration launch was definitely low. By now tempers were running very short, and not a few curses were heard at the interminable delays.

Next day the launch failed to put in an appearance, and as the day wore on hopes began to rise that they could be in for an early move. That is what happened, for just before evening the whole convoy steamed out of the estuary. By nightfall everyone not on guard had been ordered below.

The sea remained calm, and the ship responded to the gentle swell with a slight roll. Notwithstanding the lack of gale force winds, the quietness of the holds indicated the anxiety of many as to their resistance to sea-sickness. In the event these fears were groundless, and soon the swinging hammocks and creaking boards created their own soporific symphony to lull the tired men to sleep.

By morning they were well down the channel, and in the blaze of a glorious summer's day slipped uneventfully out to sea.

Sometime later someone shouted, "That's the beach-head there, right in front." Soon the decks became an anthill of curious spectators, feverishly scanning the horizon. Out of the mist the coastline suddenly hardened and came into sharp focus.

Between their ship and the shore, the spectacle which met their gaze must have been unique – ships of every shape and size, from a battleship down to a raft, were calmly riding at anchor or busily chugging shorewards. Everything seemed unnaturally peaceful; quite unlike what they had expected, even though it was almost three weeks since D day.

A naval-cutter drew alongside and an officer shouted orders to their captain through a megaphone, whereupon their ship followed the convoy to its allotted position and dropped anchor, watched intently by the crew off-watch on a nearby battleship.

The usual ribald remarks filled the air.

"The shower of blighters." fumed Morley as he leaned over the rail. "S'pose it's their night off; Saturday too. Typical Navy." He turned and addressed his audience. "It's O.K. for us to take it from them, but no one else. If it wasn't for the Navy I'd never have got away from Dunkirk – yes, we'll take it from them."

No one spoke, and all further verbal broadsides from the battleship were accepted in stoical silence – a tribute in itself to the senior service.

All that night they remained on board and despite the visit of a German aircraft, most slept like the dead.

Next day, Sunday, the beach-head looked superb in the golden sunlight. Dozens of small craft were buzzing hither and thither, going about their business of unloading. So far as the eye could see the low hills of the coastline sloped gently to the shore, and the fields behind were packed to capacity with waving corn. Undoubtedly there were devastated villages in the hinterland to tell the tale of the D-day attack, but for the moment the whole scene radiated peace.

Divine service was held later that morning, and in those momentous surroundings assumed a dignity and value a hundred times greater than mere routine observance could endow it with.

By afternoon it was the battalion's turn to unload. This coincided with the opening of a furious gun-battle somewhere over the horizon, so that their work was carried out to the cacophony of hundreds of heavy artillery field guns. The beach remained calm, but behind it an ugly monster had suddenly come to life...

Of necessity the rate of unloading was slow, and in consequence few reached the beach-head by nightfall; this resulted in further cramped sleeping quarters for the seventh successive night.

Next day unloading was speeded up by the use of large rafts, and by the afternoon the main body was ashore, despite the fact that the rafts had a top speed of only two miles-per-hour, and even that was reduced by a strong off-shore wind.

The M.T. drivers were sweating on the top line that they could achieve a dry landing on the beach. Initially the raft commander ordered them to disembark in five feet of water, but on seeing the look on their faces made a further effort and succeeded in beaching in two feet six inches of water.

Crabtree, for one, received a rude shock when he discovered his battery was flat. The leading truck was promptly ordered to tow him ashore.

The raft's ramp hit the water with a splash; Calder, Spottiswoode, and a dozen others successfully negotiated its slope, and with their engines adequately waterproofed against the shallow landing, made the shore with ease.

Poor Crabtree, awaiting his turn, said a silent prayer. The signal came, the towing-truck moved slowly towards the ramp. With fear he watched the tow-chain tighten; then he began to move. Unfortunately the raft was too short for this kind of manoeuvre – the tow-truck descended the ramp, but too slowly for Crabtree, who was tight on his tail. The momentum painstakingly gained now had to be drastically reduced; he braked. His downward rush was halted, but to no avail. As soon as the tow-truck hit the water, it accelerated. The tow-chain, of necessity very short, snapped tight and slipped free. Unable to control the momentum any further, the hapless Crabtree dropped with a mighty splash at the worst possible angle for his vehicle into the water.

"Joe Soap, that's me." he moaned, as he watched the tow-vehicle roar out of the water and onto the beach, still dragging the tow-chain.

Within minutes a bull-dozer rattled down the beach, and a fresh tow-chain was attached to Crabtree's armoured-car. Within seconds he was out, and up the beach. Another five minutes and he was in the safety of a R.E.M.E. Workshop, where he spent the next twenty-four hours drying out his engine.

Meanwhile the others pushed on at steady speed through several scarred villages, by-passed the town of Bayeux, of tapestry fame, and finally harboured in a tiny hamlet which had escaped destruction.

So it was thus that they came to Normandy, and with the deep blue sea behind them, they had only the devil in front to face.

Undoubtedly the second would prove tougher than the first.

Chapter Nine

During all this time Thorpe had been in contact with his mates only once, and that was for the few minutes when he met Percy Weatherall. For the most part he was in the dark as to their whereabouts, as they were to his.

The fact was he'd travelled over to Normandy in the same convoy as the others, in a tank-landing craft which had tacked itself onto the tail of the convoy at the last moment. He'd suffered the same amount of frustration as the others, and due to the fact that he was even more isolated he became depressed. Driven into himself he became moody, and this increased the nearer he approached foreign soil. He disembarked the day after his friends and found himself encamped at a spot several miles inland, but well clear of the front line.

It soon became obvious that the whole division was being held in reserve for a mammoth operation. The men were kept busy de-waterproofing their vehicles, and this activity was interspersed with the usual round of inspections of both vehicles and kit. They even found time for some drill and a route-march or two, but once again delay was the main order of the day.

Living inside himself, Thorpe fed on his memories. Naturally Hilary featured strongly in his thoughts, and he derived some pleasure in re-living the good times of his friendship with her. As he pondered he felt strengthened, and resolved that come what may his honour would remain untarnished, as he knew hers would be.

From his vantage point on the bridge-head Thorpe was able to note many things, including the cultivated fields of crops and vegetables, the surrounding woods filled with birdlife and flowers, all as yet untouched by the ravages of war. He took note of the French people themselves, as they went about their business as normally as possible, despite the pile of equipment and swarms of troops parked all over their properties. He was deeply impressed by their submission to the role which destiny had cast for them. He gained the impression that they had barely recovered from the shock of liberation, and that as yet their minds seemed quite incapable of taking in the details of yet another invasion. But as they had accepted and absorbed destruction in the First World War, they were again doing so now.

The imminent possibility of a disastrous defeat of the Germans by these new invaders had not, so far as he could tell, yet impinged on their thinking.

The village policeman still maintained his beat, as did the local parish priest keep watch over his flock. The farmer still made his weekly trip to Bayeux with his cart and wooden barrel, which he replenished with vin blanc.

Every farmhouse within miles of the bridge-head had its quota of refugees from the battle zone, whilst a bus ran a shuttle service to and from the front line, loaded with poor bemused wounded civilians caught up in the fighting.

Day by day the cannonade continued relentlessly, while at night the sky became alive with gun-flashes which, combined with the luminosity of the tracer bullets shooting over the beaches at the rear, made quite a lively display.

By the end of two weeks of this constant bombardment it was a miracle that neither Thorpe's faith nor will had weakened. On the contrary, his soul had been strenghtened, and this enabled him to look ahead with confidence.

He still had not made contact with his friends, and he had an idea that they would be on the look-out for him. Now it seemed certain that they would all go into battle without seeing each other.....

It was midday in the company lines. Morley was seated on an empty petrol-can sipping a mug of Copplestone's tea. By the expression on his face he was not enjoying it.

"This tea gets worse." He turned with a pained expression and stared accusingly at Copplestone.

"Not my fault, mate," Copplestone said.

"I'm not blaming you, don't get me wrong —

it's just these blooming rations, we've been on them too long without fresh food," grunted Morley.

"Too right," said Copplestone, his feelings slightly mollified. "Too much tinned food gets you down - we've had no bread since before we landed. No wonder we're all feeling weak."

They agreed...

After a while Copplestone said, his eyes shining, "I've just had an idea. If we could pound down some of these biscuits I could have a go at making pastry from the crumbs."

"It's worth a try," said Morley. "Trust you to invent a new way..." He disappeared into the rear of the section's truck and reappeared with a large tin of biscuits.

Meanwhile Copplestone scoured a nearby barn until he found what he was looking for - several pieces of wood. These he laid on the ground and covered with a ground-sheet.

Then the fun began. Morley using a shovel, and Grayson and Vincent with rifle-butts, set about crushing the hard, dry wafers. Half an hour's work yielded several mugfuls of powder.

At the end of an hour Copplestone was satisfied. He gathered up the powder, which inevitably contained a certain amount of dirt scooped up in the pounding process. He mixed the crumbs with a scrape of margarine and a drop of water, then spread it on a dixie containing shredded bully-beef. The mixture was then carefully conveyed to an earth oven, a hole in the ground with a piece of tin sticking up to serve as a chimney. The mates gathered around to assist in the stoking, and finally Copplestone pronounced the dish to be ready. He pulled it out and set it down on the ground in front of an admiring audience.

In no time the pie was polished off and everyone agreed it was an unqualified success.

"Even the tea tastes better now, you should have been a chef, mate." said Morley.

Copplestone felt suitably rewarded for his labours, and during the next few days performed wonders with his 'biscuit-pastry', manufacturing fruit and jam tarts and several more pies. In return his mates awarded him 'The Freedom of the Bridge-head'.

Of course this innovation only provided limited relief from the lack of any fresh food. The position was exacerbated by an order forbidding troops to procure food from civilians, on the basis that they required all they could grow for themselves.

One evening Weatherall strolled across from his company lines.

"How are things?" he bellowed in his usual cheery style.

"Lousy." said Morley, a disgruntled look on his face.

"Been to Bayeux yet?" Weatherall asked, changing the subject.

"No, why? It's hard enough getting our grub here without going anywhere else," Morley said.

"All the more reason for going to Bayeux - there's literally tons of food there, cheese, cream, even steak and chips."

"Steak and chips?" Morley and Copplestone said in unison.

"Yes, steak and chips, and there's no regulation to stop you buying it either."

"You're kidding, Percy." said Vincent.

"No I'm not, I had three platefuls last night, and Sawyer had two. By the way I saw Thorpe in Bayeux last night, in a steak and chip cafe. He wants to meet you there to-morrow afternoon outside the cathedral."

"Saw Arthur, did you?" asked Grayson, who had joined the group. "In a steak and chip cafe? How come, you weren't in England?"

"No, no," laughed Weatherall, "on this very bridge-head. Be at Bayeux Cathedral to-morrow afternoon at 1600 hours, and you'll see for yourself."

The news soon spread through the battalion, and although it was viewed with some scepticism everyone not on duty determined to make the expedition.

Next afternoon the procession began, and all along the four mile route it was joined by dozens of Tommies from a hundred different units. By the time they reached Bayeux the road was jammed with soldiers, all laughing and shouting, and quite oblivious to the battle-front so near at hand, or to the Luftwaffe, who were still very much in evidence.

All other roads converging on Bayeux were similarly crammed, and within an hour the town was filled with a living mass of khaki.

"Just like York on Saturday afternoons," said Henshaw, as he pushed his way through the throng.

"Right." muttered Grayson.

"Keep going straight, then turn right at the end of the street, the cathedral is somewhere there," said Henshaw.

Eventually they arrived, but there was no sign of Thorpe.

"It's after four o'clock, better give him a few minutes," Grayson said.

Shortly afterwards Thorpe arrived, puffing and panting from his struggle through the crowds.

"Sorry I'm late, lads, it's great to see you all again." He smiled, and shook hands.

Henshaw and Grayson beamed at him like two schoolboys. They plied each other with questions for twenty minutes, comparing notes about their movements since leaving Yorkshire.

Eventually Henshaw said, "One of the reaons we've come to-day is that there's a strong rumour circulating that there's a steak and ship cafe here."

"Sure is, in fact there are several. I'll take you," said Thorpe.

They pushed their way down several alleys where the crowd was thinnest, and made for a cafe. Outside was a long queue of soldiers patiently waiting; all the cafes in the town had similar queues — indeed that was the easiest method of recognising them.

"This is hopeless, we'll be here all day at this rate," said Grayson.

"Never fear, the queue soon disappears. You see the cafes hold roughly twenty-five people, and 'Le Patron' lets that number in at any given time. Then the doors are locked, and they're served, and so on..." Thorpe said knowledgeably.

Grayson counted sixty bodies in front of them.

"That'll mean we're in the third lot, in three quarters of an hour's time." he said, his voice crestfallen.

Eventually, unbelievably, it was their turn, and they sank their teeth into real steak. They could hardly believe it, and ate in silence. They washed the spread down with a cup of coffee, and rose to let the next lot in.

"Boy, that was good – I feel like a giant refreshed," said Grayson rubbing his stomach.

Outside, they caught sight of Cragg and Hilton, sipping a pale beverage out of tiny mugs, in a shop.

"What on earth's that?" said Henshaw.

"Cream." said Thorpe.

They went into the shop, laughing.

Once inside they sampled some cream themselves, and were just about to leave the shop when they saw Weatherall, Sawyer, and several others, carrying a pile of large round Bayeux cheeses.

"Where did you get those?" asked Henshaw.

"Next street; you can get as much as you like – what did I tell you?" chuckled Weatherall.

They changed roles; Percy and his group supped the cream, while the others set off in search of the cheese.

"Ask for 'fromage'," Weatherall shouted after them.

They bought several cheeses, then headed for the cathedral. Here they saw a replica of the famous Bayeux tapestry, which hung in a room near the entrance.

Finally, having satiated themselves on the treasures inside the cathedral – which miraculously had escaped bomb damage – they found themselves in the street once more. By now it was early evening, and their stomachs said they could toy with some more steak. Accordingly, they made for another cafe, and tagged themselves on to the end of the queue.

This time they had to wait for an hour and a half, and even then were still some way from the door when, to their horror, a notice appeared stating the shop was closing at nine o'clock.

Panic set in, which resulted in the queue breaking up and being replaced by a similar number of determined customers crowding the door.

The friends stood their ground, till finally, frustrated beyond limits of human endurance, the crowd turned into a human battering-ram and charged. Momentarily they jammed the doorway, till someone managed to free himself, and several dozen soldiers were forced inside.

Counting in French, Le Patron pronounced that he had the twenty-five, and shut the door amidst howls of protest.

The five friends were lucky, as they managed to end up the right side of the door – but only just.

Once more full to the brim with steak, they set off for their respective camps, but not before they all agreed to meet again on Monday for a similar feast.

The only thing which took the gilt off the ginger-bread and spoiled a superb day was the discovery, when each of them opened his parcel of steak which he'd purchased for taking back to camp, that it had gone bad.

It was not till several weeks later that a possible answer to the riddle of the bad meat was discovered. By then they'd had time to notice the considerable number of dead cattle lying around the battlefield. This, they decided, could have been the reason for the glut of meat in Bayeux at that time.

The day following the visit to Bayeux, their waiting-time at the bridge-head came to an end. Within minutes came the sudden order to move, and within an hour the whole battalion was on its way to take its place in the order of battle.

It was two days later when they received the official briefing for the attack. The company commander was at pains to point out that they would not be involved in 'the big break-out', but rather they would be employed in diversionary tactics, in an attempt to lure enemy forces to their front, and their advance was only to penetrate for about seven miles.

All visions of a drive through to Paris vanished, and the faces of the men fell.

They spent the remainder of that day in quiet preparation for the offensive.

****

The roar of hundreds of four-engined bombers at 06.30 hours the following morning told the division that its hour of battle had arrived. This awe-inspiring sight had barely passed overhead before the mouths of hundreds of guns opened up, belching flame.

This time the focal point was a bridge near the ancient town of Caen. The place had been reached only after a dreadful night drive, where the Normandy dust coupled with the blackout had turned the journey into a nightmare, and where only iron discipline, constantly sustained, ensured that they got there at all.

They watched an allied plane being hit, and disintegrate in flames.

"Jerry's fighting back, he's fighting back." someone shouted.

During the next three hours relays of medium bombers carried out further attacks. Troops, who were awaiting their turn to attack, hurriedly ate a hastily prepared breakfast, then mounted their vehicles and sat nervously fingering their weapons, or relaxing, trying to shake off some of the effects of the night drive.

Suddenly the signal to start engines was given, and men dashed to their trucks. Slowly at first, they moved, then faster and faster. They crossed a road, came onto an open space littered with the wreckage of D-day glider landings, passed through the gun-lines, descended a ravine, crossed a couple of pontoon-bridges, and entered the smoke of a dozen wrecked villages, surrounded by fields of corn, all being torn apart by bursting shells and vehicle tracks.

An allied fighter plane, badly hit, burst into

flames as it hit the ground fifty yards in front of them.

The German artillery began to home in on them, and some near hits ranged around the column. Their pace had slackened to a crawl, which made them easy targets. Faces became drawn and white; few words were spoken.

Then they halted – right in the open fields. There was no cover, so they deployed quickly and expertly. An infantry brigade marched through the centre of them and started digging in a little way ahead.

Presently a tank was hit, and caught fire. Armoured stretcher-bearer cars and several jeeps moved backwards and forwards, in and out, of the countless number of battle-wagons strewn across the fields.

A considerable force was obviously being employed in the attack, and it began to dawn on the friends that they were, as yet, still very much second fiddle in the general scheme of things.

Presently there was a lull, and the sun, which had been hidden behind the pall of gun-smoke, showed itself momentarily. Men relaxed cautiously, but not for long, for suddenly a hideous, squealing, soul-petrifying sound pierced their ear-drums. Only a few knew what it meant, but instantly, to a man they all did the same thing, and took cover, piling out of the trucks and dropping flat to the ground, hugging it close to them while salvoes of 'minnenwerfers' crashed around them.

"Moaning Minnies" bawled Crabtree, jumping to his feet. "Boy, you're looking white about the gills, Joe." he glanced in Spottiswoode's direction.

"Cor, that nearly blew my boots off. Did you ever hear such a noise?" said the shaken Spottiswoode between his teeth.

These terrible attacks were repeated several times before the order to advance was given. When it did they progressed in fits and starts, as several small woods had to be cleared on the way. Eventually all opposition was disposed of and they arrived on the outskirts of their objectives.

Again there was a lull; the din lessened. Once again everyone became fidgety. Several civilians, who had braved the fearful barrage, trudged past them ·to the safety of the British lines.

"Let's get on; can't stand this delay," hissed Crabtree, as he peered through the vizor of his armoured-car.

"Ah, here we go," he muttered to himself, as the ·vehicles in front eased forward. The pace quickened. Grayson tailed Crabtree, who in turn tailed Spottiswoode, each vehicle keeping its proper distance.

They entered the village, or what was left of it. It had already been cleared, so they pushed on down the road and halted, while some tanks in front assaulted a wood.

There was no sign of the enemy, but a reconnaissance patrol did encounter some scattered infantry further down the road. The attack edged forward cautiously, but the enemy had become impatient. From a wood in front a bright yellow-red flash and a loud report betrayed their presence. With the speed of lightning the company dived out of the trucks once more, and into ditches, while the tanks concentrated on a speedy withdrawal.

Shrapnel spattered in all directions; a tank caught a direct hit. A grenade dropped in the road, followed by a smoke shell. Then the field-grey uniforms of the enemy could be seen as they doubled towards the cover of a hedgerow. Speedy orders from the company commander ensured that the platoons took up defensive positions, where they opened up on the Germans with small-arms fire, forcing them to withdraw.

However the British advance had reached its limit, the seven miles had been covered, and night was approaching. The troops fell into defensive positions around the village. As darkness fell the gun-fire gradually ceased and a deadly stillness took over. This was broken only occasionally by an isolated shot, indicating that patrols were active on both sides.

Some distance to the rear a red glare lit up

the sky. It was too close to come from the beaches, yet was in the direction from which the attack had been launched that morning. Soon the tell-tale noise of aircraft engines overhead returning from a mission gave the clue.

At dawn Calder brought the details; he'd been back to 'Div' in his jeep.

"The rear echelons copped it proper last night, though I don't think any of our chaps were hurt. At any rate I saw Henshaw and Phelps, they were both O.K.," he said.

"Anyone seen Thorpe?" Grayson queried.

"No," said Calder.

"Keep a look-out for him if you go back."

"O.K.," said Calder.

By this time the sun was rising, and with it the artillery on both sides opened up. The friends' unit was in the middle of it all as the barrage from both sides passed overhead. The bombardment varied from 'Moaning Minnies' to the occasional air-burst, then a full air-raid thrown in for good measure.

All that day was spent in the slit-trenches; so was the next. Heavy rain added to the discomfort. By the third day no one was particularly lively. By now the shelling had become almost continuous. Crabtree got caught in the open and received a shrapnel-wound in his leg, becoming the first casualty of the group.

The Quartermaster issued the rum-ration, and this served to help keep up the morale. One teetotal soldier looked so miserable that his sergeant ordered him to drink a large tot.

The result was the youngster lost all sense of responsibility, jumped out of the trench, and wandered about, oblivious to the bombardment. It took several stentorian bellows from the sergeant to restore him to his senses.

Next day they were relieved and drove back to the suburbs of Caen, which had been devastated by the bombing. Nevertheless it seemed like heaven compared to the front-line they'd just left, and despite nocturnal visits by the Luftwaffe and some isolated shelling by day, they set up home in the damaged buildings.

Once they were called upon for a further attack, but it was called off before they had a chance to engage the enemy, who had been tricked into drawing his main force to the Caen front.

That day the Americans broke through. So the battalion's aim - their holding and delaying tactics - had been achieved.

Several days later they returned to the Bayeux area from where they had started out so confidently only a week before. The wounded Crabtree was evacuated to England, much to the envy of all.

That night, after a 'brew-up', Copplestone said, "My main worry now is what to tell the wife. She'd be scared stiff if she knew the truth."

"Tell her you've been playing cricket on the bridge-head," grinned Vincent.

"Do you think she'd believe it?"

"Try it anyway."

He did.

Chapter Ten

Their rest period was just twelve hours old when the order came to prepare to move in an hour's time. Calder was detailed to leave in fifteen minutes by jeep with the advance party.

A short briefing followed in which they were informed of their new objective, an insignificant looking place on the map. To add to their gloom, the company commander mentioned that they could expect to encounter opposition before the position was reached. The platoon commanders and sergeants were briefed separately, and from them the other ranks gained the picture. Things were on the move, and very much in the Allies' favour, for in addition to the superb American break-out, the Second British Army had started to roll back the enemy. Their division was to make a valuable contribution to this success.

Grayson's depression had reached an all-time low, and as the column again set off on its tedious journey his face was pale and glum. The moon was full, and as darkness fell the stars twinkled bravely, endeavouring to transmit their message of cheer to the frustrated soldiers.

The column by-passed sleeping Bayeux, turned left along a first class road, and kept up a steady pace for about an hour. They then moved onto a second class road. The drivers were just beginning to compliment themselves on their good fortune in having such excellent night driving conditions when suddenly they turned again, this time on to a narrow lane, bounded on either side by thick hedgerows.

It wasn't long before the tank tracks and wheels of the other vehicles began to throw up dust into thick clouds, as grim as any London fog, successfully blocking all driver vision. Soon the moon and stars became lost to view, and in order to see the tail-light of the vehicle in front, each driver was compelled to close up the distance. In this manner they crawled along mile after mile, twisting and turning through a labyrinth of lanes and tracks.

At 0100 the second drivers relieved their

comrades for a short spell, while the latter attempted to free themselves of the layer of dust which had accumulated in eyes, noses and mouths, and which clung in incredible quantities to their clothes.

Finally the column halted in some orchards, and the opportunity to breathe some fresh air was siezed.

Calder appeared out of the darkness.

"Well old son of a gun, how long have you been waiting for us?" enquired Copplestone.

"Hours; but you aren't stopping here, you merchants."

"Why?" a chorus of voices.

"Because we've had orders to push on, that's why." he retorted, with an edge to his voice. "We've another five miles to go before we harbour for the night."

"For the night? It'll be morning by then," sneered Vincent.

The order to start up was given, and in a few minutes the orchards were empty. Visibility improved considerably, but because it was by now 0300 hours, fatigue remained acute, and the night seemed endless. The effort to keep awake became nothing short of a fight for survival.

Finally they approached their harbouring area, which turned out to be a cornfield surrounded by trees, under whose shelter they flung themselves down in a desperate attempt to snatch an hour's sleep.

Again their hopes were dashed, for within a short while the woods in front became alive with the resounding boom of concentrated gun-fire. Apparently they had harboured behind the gun-lines, and were not intended to rest. There they remained all the next day, and as the gun-fire drifted further and further away, the terrible anticipation of another night drive to catch up with the advance descended upon all like some fearful black blanket.

At dusk this feeling was translated into fact, and in the fading twilight they were drawn up in order of battle. This time they were assembled in a new order; a company of infantry with a squadron of tanks – a fresh formation learnt from the bitter fighting around Caen.

"There's already a group up front," said Calder. "We're in luck; we won't go into the attack now till morning."

"Yes, but our platoon's in the van of our group, don't forget," a voice piped up out of the darkness.

The column moved, and the detestable dust instantly moved with it, billowing around the vehicles for all the world like a desert sand storm.

The route lay through fields, down the centre of which a track had been marked with white tape, only just visible. The track was well worn, and studded with ruts and hollows. They bounced over these and eventually exited onto a narrow road along which they careered for some distance till they entered the remains of a small village, whose bomb-blasted houses presented a grim spectacle silhouetted against the back-cloth of gun-flashes. Smoke and the smell of charred buildings hung heavy in the air, and the solitary road was littered with wreckage; but through it all they tore; then just as suddenly halted, and harboured again.

The guns continued to work overtime as the company hastily dug their slit-trenches, urged on by the fearsome screech of the 'Moaning Minnies'. After a time these became less frequent, and by the time the weary men fell into the trenches at 0400 hours, exhaustion was so complete that nothing could keep them awake.

It seemed they had barely blinked their eyes before it was dawn, and with it came the relentless order to start-up. Down the road they moved, more asleep than awake, and by the look on their faces most of the men still imagined it was all part of their nightmare. A mixture of smoke and mist blotted out the landscape in front, and raised hopes that their dawn move would be screened from the enemy.

The countryside through which they now moved was heavily wooded, for they had penetrated that part of Normandy known as the Bocage, which with its leafy lanes, abundance of trees and hedgerows, and acre upon acre of cornfields, could look quite delightful in a different setting. But to an invading force every hillock could spell death.

They consolidated their position in yet another devastated village, took up defensive positions, and awaited the order to push on once more. A unit in front was already in the throes of assaulting a wooded ridge beyond the village, and as this would take sometime there was ample time in which to dig trenches and cook breakfast. These tasks were accomplished amidst a salvo of 'Moaning Minnies', which luckily didn't do any damage. However no one was in any doubt that they were under enemy observation.

Fed and watered, they fumed in their trenches while the Germans set about creating as much havoc as possible, including constant harassment by sniper fire. Poor Calder was forced to run the gauntlet of all this in his jeep several times during the course of the day. At one stage things were so bad that every time a soldier moved in the slit-trench the enemy retaliated with a fusillade of small-arms fire.

The only other cover offered in the village, apart from the trenches, was a solitary house, as yet undamaged, and this soon became home for a section headed by Calder, who were prepared to take their chance above ground rather than in a trench.

Inside the men piled the scanty furniture into the doorway in an attempt to form a barricade against enemy attack. By midday the incessant shelling was beginning to have its effect on morale.

"I thought we were suppposed to attack?" queried a nervous looking Vincent.

"So we were, those others in front must have slowed down," said an ashen Calder.

"Things aren't going too well," muttered Copplestone.

"He was only stating what was already in all their minds, and thereafter they lapsed into silence, their faces portraying their feelings.

63

Even Calder's indomitable spirit had gone. As trained soldiers they were still game, but they were coming to the end of their endurance - something would have to happen soon.

Grayson suggested a prayer. To this they all readily agreed. He said one in his faltering fashion, and they all felt the better for it.

As the day wore on the bombardment lessened, until as if in answer to their prayer, it died away altogether. By nightfall all was calm, and the men responded favourably to the order to remain in their positions over-night - suddenly the impossibility of a full night's sleep had turned into a probability.

They moved with the dawn. The village was still wreathed in smoke as the men weaved their way out of the debris. There had been no time to wash or eat.

The road took a dip, then turned up a steep slope. Half-way up this they halted for a breather.

"This must be the place that other unit was held up at yesterday," said Copplestone.

"Yeah, looks like it, there's some of them over there," said Vincent.

In the dell were a number of men and vehicles. One of the men approached.

"How yah?" said Grayson.

"O.K. now; but you see yesterday - oh boy." the soldier shrugged and waved his hand towards the summit of the slope. "Yesterday morning this place was a hell on earth, we lost a lot of good men and tanks trying to take it. Jerry was holed up in all that growth, tanks and all. He waited till we were thirty yards away, then let us have it."

Grayson's eyebrows raised.

"By midday we had it under control, and were able to push on."

Grayson looked at his mates; they were thinking... 'midday yesterday, we had it under control...'. He couldn't help wondering if there was some divine connection, for just after his prayer things had got better for them as well at midday yesterday.

"See over there," the soldier went on, "that's a dry-well. We found a family of civilians there, crouched inside they were, with a thumping great stone on the top -scared stiff from all the shelling. Didn't even know the battle was over till we found them."

"Poor blighters, civvies always get the worst of it in these conditions," sympathised Copplestone.

They moved on up the slope, where yet another burning village met their eyes. On they pushed, without pausing, and presently entered another village which with the exception of its church had escaped unscathed. A huge burnt-out tiger tank was slumped across the road in front of the church. Further on up the road the leading vehicles could be seen moving into the fields.

Shortly afterwards, with the arrival of the rest of the formation, the order to prepare for attack was given. After a hasty check of vehicles and weapons they moved on. Two formations of their own group had turned left shortly before, so they took the right fork, which led down into a ravine. At the bottom they crossed a small bridge which spanned a pretty river. In peace-time it would have been an ideal spot for a picnic, but now the air was charged with death, as bursting shells and mortars spilled their contents over everything.

Of necessity their progress was snail-like. Painfully they ascended the far side of the ravine by a track through a wood, and crossed several fields and then, rather than expose the vehicles to any further enemy fire from over the crest, the company commander ordered them to halt and take up defensive positions beside several hedgerows. The sections de-bussed and moved forward on foot, laden with bren-guns, Piats, and ammunition. Oatley's platoon led, Cragg's followed, and Vincent and Copplestone brought up the rear, while the drivers remained behind with their vehicles.

So far not a man had fallen. But the enemy was playing a clever game; no sooner had the sections departed than a murderous concentration of fire dropped on the stationary vehicles.

Calder and company took cover over the brow of a hill, but immediately came under sniper fire, and for some minutes were pinned down. Soon afterwards an officer and a soldier from the battalion were wounded, and a stretcher-bearer dashed to their aid.

Their position was weighted heavily in the enemy's favour, so a general evacuation was ordered to a less exposed ravine. For the rest of that day the enemy pumped round after round of accurate gun-fire over men and vehicles.

Meanwhile the forward sections were pushing across country. Several large woods on the sky-line were the objectives. By the time they had cleared a route and doubled across numerous fields they all felt punctured. As soon as the first wood was reached enemy machine-gun fire came from everywhere, despite the fact that the sections had already surprised several machine-gunners before they could fire. The wood seemed endless, but at last, panting with exertion, Oatley's platoon, which was leading, was through it. Mortar bombs began to drop like hail around them.

The arrival of Cragg's platoon at the wood brought the forward platoon some relief, as for a while the enemy gunners concentrated on this new platoon. The others came abreast, and they were about to move forward in a joint operation, when the dreaded shout of 'Panzers' rent the air.

In a dip in front, several tanks and tracked vehicles were seen moving towards them. Then others appeared behind. To advance, or even remain where they were, would be suicide; so a hasty withdrawal was ordered. Eventually they managed to retreat to a captured farm, where they met up with the other platoons. Soon enemy machine-guns became trained on the farmhouse, and to all intents and purposes, they appeared to be surrounded.

They were eternally grateful for several bren-carriers which did yeoman service in holding off Jerry. One carrier lost a track, which the driver replaced with the enemy literally yards away; while his crew wasted no time in shooting up some German infantry, who were attempting to filter through unnoticed.

Finally, to avoid complete encirclement, the company was ordered to withdraw to a spur half a mile back. This, despite their fatigue, they accomplished in good order.

Packed with troops, the bren-carriers, despite their extra burden, never faltered, and thanks mainly to their efforts, everyone reached the spur without further casualties. Having reached the spur, which was where they'd left the transport that morning, they were bitterly disappointed not to find the vehicles waiting.

"That means no grub either; all our rations were on the trucks." groaned Cragg.

Once again they 'dug-in', and as the ground was like concrete, this was an ordeal in itself.

By nightfall there was still no sign of the transport. As night took a grip the battle-noises died away, and the stillness was only broken by the constant rasping of shovels on hard ground, as men fought to increase the depth of the trenches. Sweating, panting, cursing, they worked. The stars came out and the moon turned the velvet darkness into something approaching daylight. All around, the cornfields lay white and still.

"Listen." someone said.

Everyone strained his ears.

"Jerry?" someone else said.

"No, it's the transport." Cragg shouted in sheer relief.

Across the ravine they heard the rumble of engines. Loudly they roared closer.

"They'll give our positions away for sure." fumed a sergeant.

On they came, their engines revving like tractors, and finally halted in the field beside the company.

Willing hands helped to unload rations, but they were not permitted to eat in peace, for suddenly out of the gloom a grenade exploded near one of the advance posts. Several men were wounded, but much to their relief it was not followed by any further 'fireworks'.

For what remained of the night half the company rested, while the other half kept guard. The company commander inspected the wounded, and told Fanshawe, the most badly wounded one, that he would be going back to England.

Copplestone and Grayson, who were standing within earshot, found it difficult to control their envy, and were glad that the night hid their expressions.

"England, old England," sighed Grayson to himself wondering if he would ever see it again – it seemed ten thousand miles away at that moment. His mind focused on Aunt Elizabeth; would she pray for him? He took a long, hard look at the stars, and knew that the answer was – yes.

Grayson was ordered to evacuate the wounded. He jumped into his truck and started up, his reserve driver at his side. Together they tore off into the darkness, leaving Copplestone and the rest expecting every minute to be shelled, because of the noise of his engine; but nothing happened.

The church in the village was still smouldering from the bombardment the morning before.

Grayson pointed out a small cottage close to it. "You weren't with us this afternoon" he turned to his relief, "the transport was ordered back from the ravine, because we heard you were all surrounded. That's why you missed us, but when we passed that house some 'Moaning Minnies' dropped too close for comfort, so we all dived for shelter. Some French civilians beckoned me into that cottage, and I made it just in time. Amid all the din one old woman shouted, 'Le grand jour de liberation.'" Grayson shook his head in wonder. "They've waited for this day for so long, and it's come with such noise and destruction, but their spirit is marvellous."

They completed their errand and began the return journey. All went well till they were within a few hundred yards of their location, when a flare went up to their right.

They held their breath, fearing another bombardment, but none came. They wasted no time in diving into their trench.

Due to their exposed position, an elaborate guard system had to be effected, and due to the exhausted state of the men, the sentries changed every hour on the hour. It seemed to Oatley that he had barely closed his eyes when he was shaken into life for his turn. He adjusted his steel helmet and took up his position behind a bren-gun facing into the darkness. He could see the guard corporal some ten yards away in the gloom, but the moment was too grim for conversation. Oatley imagined that every shadow hid a German, and any rustle in the cornfields signified a sniper's nest. After a while weird shapes danced before his eyes. Several times he was overcome with exhaustion and had to force himself to stay awake.

Dawn found the whole company, without exception, drawn and desperately weary. But if they had hoped for relief with the coming of daylight they were to be disappointed.

The tank squadron was just forming up and the infantry had just started to move in the slit-trenches, when the sky filled with shells, and for fifteen minutes they had to endure a bombardment so accurate that no one dared raise his head. It was obvious that their position had been marked with considerable accuracy and that an attack in strength was imminent.

Then the barrage slackened, but only to reveal the fields alive with field-grey uniforms. These were accompanied by a hail of machine-fun fire, whilst mortar bombs and grenades rained down on the unfortunate men in the trenches.

Oatley felt a sudden surge of power; if ever he was glad of all his past hard training, it was now.

The tank crews, realising the disadvantage the men in the trenches found themselves in, opened up with all they had, causing the enemy to hesitate momentarily, but it was just long enough to allow the company to recover itself and to enable them to return fire. Oatley's bren-gun began to spit bullets, and as fast as he emptied one magazine his mate was at hand with a fresh one. It was warm work, but they were now firing with effect, so much so that Jerry decided not to close in for the kill. Those in the field-grey uniforms still alive hurriedly retired, or stayed hidden in the cornfields, parts of which had already caught fire from the tracer bullets.

German artillery continued to shell the spur unceasingly, and for the next few hours the ground was ploughed up, chewed up, rocked and torn to shreds by heavy explosive shells, with an occasional armour-piercer thrown in for good measure.

By now the sun was high in the sky, and the company was able to give some attention to the position it was holding, which the men had been either too occupied or too tired to do the previous evening. It happened to be in the centre of a potato field, which was the only one in the area; so Copplestone, with his usual foresight, was not long about filling several sandbags full; this would make a welcome variation in the section's diet. As he was forced to stand up to perform his task, and thus expose himself to enemy snipers, he was roundly applauded when he'd completed the job unharmed -- indeed this defiant gesture was just what the lads needed.

An increase in the volume of the enemy's fire heralded the beginning of their second attack, and this proved to be even more determined than the first. It was delivered by infantry, supported by tanks. In the process Oatley's bren-gun became red-hot, but still Jerry advanced until the leading tank was barely seventy yards away. Its commander didn't lack courage, for his voice was clearly audidble urging his infantry forward, and hurling curses at the 'insignificant British'. His words added the touch-paper to the fanaticism of the young S.S.troops, who rushed the British line.

Oatley's platoon was still more or less intact, but in Cragg's a number of casualties had already occurred, and it looked as if they must be over-run. But, as is often the case, the hour produced the man, for a corporal near Cragg jumped into a truck in full view of the advancing enemy, turned its Browning gun in their direction, and emptied a belt of ammunition at the tank. All this was done despite a murderous hail of enemy bullets which burst into the sides of his vehicle. Another N.C.O. coolly aimed a rifle shot at the tank-commander, wounding him, so that he dropped inside his turret, but came up again like a brave jack-in-the-box, only to perish as the same marksman found his brain.

By this time the tank was less than forty yards away and still advancing – another minute, and Cragg and his section would be crushed like eggs in a box. Suddenly, unbelievably, Cragg saw one of those terrible tracks fall apart. The monster gave a lurch, half-turned, then stopped. The crew baled out and disappeared like rabbits into the cornfields.

"Well done there." shouted an officer.

Cragg turned his head to see two grimy faces beaming all over with pride, as they crouched beside their PIAT gun, which they had, with no small risk to themselves, used against the enemy with such devastating effect.

With basic training asserting itself, Cragg from his trench, and Oatley from his, again prepared to fire, but the need had disappeared. It appeared that the single bomb from the PIAT had the same effect on Jerry as the stone from David's sling had on the Philistines. Within a matter of minutes all enemy tanks had withdrawn over the crest of the hill, leaving behind their heavy artillery to rake the British position.

With this sustained fire it was inevitable that the casualties mounted in the company, and within a short space of time several tanks and trucks were hit. As they became engulfed by flames the exploding ammunition they carried caused further casualties.

The sun, like a foretaste of Doomsday, assumed a dark smoke-tinged halo. By now it was midday, and many cups of tea appeared from nowhere. There still weren't enough to go around, so everyone had to be content with sips.

"We still haven't achieved much of a breakthrough," Vincent said to Copplestone.

"No, and it's about time we were relieved, something's wrong," Copplestone replied.

"Bet you a fiver Jerry's jammed our radio. No messages in, no messages out. No wonder we've not been relieved," Vincent said with fear mounting in his voice.

His observations were very close to the truth, and as the day wore on, this became apparent. Casualties in both men and vehicles continued to mount.

An N.C.O. said, "We must keep this road open at all costs, there's several battalions still to come through."

By now they were desperately short of ammunition, so a troop of bren-carriers was dispatched for more. A number of wounded were packed into these vehicles, and they set off at high speed before the enemy could range on them.

Late in the afternoon the enemy attacked again, and at sunset the sky once more rained shells. Yet again their isolated company had to watch the field-grey uniforms advancing through the cornfields, only to find the trenches still fiercely defended. Ammunition stocks replenished, the defenders kept up a steady fire which eventually depleted the German numbers, and broke up the advance. A few brave ones continued to press forward, but never reached the hedgerows, which continued to remain British property.

Their advance broken, the enemy retreated, and in minutes calm reigned. The German infantry appeared to evaporate whence they came, but their artillery still continued to shell the position till well on into the night.

Another night's vigil commenced.

****

At dawn word was passed around that they were to be relieved. Unbelievably, a scout car drove up - they were to be relieved by a Highland Regiment.

Calder was waiting for them at their new harbouring area. He'd missed most of the recent action as he'd been sent on a mission the previous night. Now he stood by his jeep, an enormous grin splitting his face.

"Well done lads," he chuckled as the trucks passed him, and parked in a field, "all joking apart, you all look ten years older."

After the chore of digging the slit-trenches was complete, the men gathered into groups to swap stories about their recent experiences. As usual Calder held the largest audience. He mentioned that he'd been back to 'Div' and seen Thorpe. Everyone there had heard of the company's 'back to the wall' stand...they had made their name.

Next day the Mobile Bath Unit arrived in the area, so it wasn't long before a number of customers set off in trucks to locate it. They found the unit, which had set up operations by the river in the very ravine where the transport had endured grim shelling earlier on. Now all looked peaceful and green, bathed in sunlight, and showing little sign of that dreadful situation.

"By the way, what's this place called?" Morley asked.

"Dashed if I know," said Calder, vainly consulting a map.

"Let's call it the 'Spud Patch'," sniggered Vincent.

Ever afterwards, when speaking of the particular action, the members of the company referred to it as 'The Spud Patch'.

Later that afternoon the order to move was again passed around. This was cancelled at the last minute, and instead the company was treated to an entire afternoon's artillery entertainment by several batteries of self-propelled guns, lodged in the next field.

That evening the Padre conducted a service in the field, and of all the events of that terrible week, it proved the most moving. The desperately worn faces of the men, the background noise of heavy artillery, devastation on all sides for as far as the eye could see, all bathed in the red/yellow glow of the setting sun, produced a deep emotional effect in each man.

The next day was August 7th – that great day in the Normandy Campaign.

73

'Prepare to move'. The words were repeated from platoon to platoon. They moved with considerable consternation. Jerry was retaliating in dead earnest, and was putting in a fierce attack on the American forces at Mortain, which, by reason of its proximity to the British front, augured badly for allied support troops.

Down yet another country lane they rattled, fearful lest their dust should attract enemy attention, finally arriving in an orchard. Typhoons and Thunderbolts in their scores roared overhead, bent on death dealing activities towards the advancing foe. Their success in this action is now part of history, with the result that the company slept well that night, and were left in peace for the next two days.

Eagerly they filled this unbelievably pleasant vacuum with rest and recreational activities, such as catching up with their letters home.

"Listen mate," Copplestone chuckled to Vincent, a letter in his hand. "You remember I wrote to my wife saying I was playing cricket on the bridge-head?"

Vincent nodded, a grin starting to spread.

"Well, she says she's glad I've got such a good job out here, and she hopes my billet's comfortable."

Copplestone threw the letter in the air and both men burst into hysterical laughter.

"I can hardly believe it." Copplestone howled, and laughed and hugged himself till the tears ran down his face. "Anyway," he finally said, "I'm glad she's not worrying over me, I'll put her wise one day."

"An anti-tank gun platoon was posted into the company, and Grayson noted it was Sawyer's. It seemed an age since they'd met, although they had rarely been more than a few hundred yards away from each other during the campaign. They were given little opportunity to fraternise, for almost straight away they were detailed to take over a freshly captured position from some infantry.

Within the hour the column was climbing out of the hollow up a slope, the sound of battle getting louder.

"They reckon the road's under observation. That means our dust trails'll bring Jerry," said Morley comfortingly.

They harboured in another orchard. Then tension became agonising; shells bracketed them. Swiftly they made use of some enemy-dug trenches.

'Start-up' came the order, just as they were feeling safe.

"We're going by a lower road," said a sergeant, "but we'll be lucky to get there."

They moved at a mere crawl for half-a-mile, then turned off onto a road which was in the process of being mercilessly bombarded. The enemy appeared to be concentrating on a bridge which had to be crossed. How they wished the pace would quicken; instead it slackened until, just as the van of the column reached the bridge, it stopped altogether.

"This is it." said Morley, pointing, white as a sheet. "Vehicles jammed in the road. We're in God's hands now."

Unashamedly, Grayson dropped his head and prayed as he sat at the wheel of his vehicle. Presently he stepped onto the road, where he joined Morley. So far the shells were falling wide of the mark - but it was only a matter of time. With considerable relief they saw the head of the column begin to move. Back in their vehicles they fumed at the slowness of it all. For sure they must be sitting ducks.

Inch by inch they crawled along till they finally reached their next harbouring area. Not a moment too soon; as a rush of air shells whizzed past their vehicles, descending on the bridge they'd just left.

"It's a miracle," muttered Morley, "it's nothing short of a miracle."

Sawyer joined them. He seemed in particularly good heart, and it transpired that he'd just received a magazine from home "mentioning him in dispatches". It also mentioned he'd become the proud father of a baby son, since his arrival in Normandy. The serious business of yet more trench-digging aborted much congratulation from his friends, and although the front was by now quiet, all were on the alert.

At dusk the cooks from company headquarters arrived and made a hot meal. Afterwards they settled in for another night of waiting. It became very easy for them to be lured into a sense of false security on such a night, when deathly stillness took over. But they all knew their courage would be tested again in the morning.

Sure enough, a barrage from the British artillery heralded the dawn. Taking up action stations for the umpteenth time that week, they watched Weatherall's company move out in front.

"They'll be second in, and we're last," said Morley, who as usual had all the answers.

Weatherall's company was the pride of the battalion, and on that perfect August morning they locked superb. Doubtless internally they didn't feel the same confidence which they gave to the rest of the battalion that day.

Several hundred yards down the road they halted. A party of blood-stained men passed them, heading in the opposite direction, an indication that the leading company had already engaged the enemy. Presently reports filtered through that a minefield had been encountered on a bridge over a small stream, and that after losing several men and tanks, the remainer of the platoons had forded the stream lower down, and had gone forward on foot across fields to rendezvous at a crossroads.

A further batch of wounded appeared and said that they had followed the infantry across fields in an armoured-car, all the time being mercilessly shelled. Near the crossroads their vehicle had received a direct hit, and they had left it burning like a bonfire. They were unable to give any further information on the forward platoons. Messages that were received indicated an enormous number of snipers everywhere, many armed with bazookas and mortars, all accurately sited on the bridge, turning it into a virtual death trap. Even stretcher-bearer waggons were not immune from this hail of death.

Weatherall's company waited. An hour went by

with no further progress. Finally a single bren-carrier came tearing towards them. As it passed, it slowed, allowing its crew to deliver the latest information. They'd just returned from the forward platoons, running the gauntlet of the barrage in order to bring back wounded and up to date information, and to re-stock with ammunition. They said the platoons in the village ahead had suffered heavy casualties, and were now effectively held down by the enemy. Many tanks had been hit and knocked out of the action. Accelerating, the bren-carrier drove on to complete its mission.

Wounded men continued to dribble back. Some had been involved in a successful attack on a small hamlet to the left of the main line of advance. Others had been on the bridge, which they said was in the process of being cleared of mines despite the devastating fire. One man admitted he'd been so dazed that he found himself bandaging up the dead instead of the wounded.

Some time later the same bren-carrier reappeared with a full load of wounded, and informed Weatherall that by now the remnants of the forward platoons had been reinforced by tanks, and that one had already been put out of action. Snipers had the village at their mercy, and any time now the enemy were expected to take it.

Weatherall's company was ordered to start up. Slowly they moved down a second class road, screened by orchards and woods. A mile further on they were ordered to de-bus, and moved forward on foot, weapons at the ready. The road took a sudden dip into a gully, and at the bottom they saw the fateful bridge. Cautiously they approached, and when only a few yeards from it were ordered to take cover. Within minutes tanks and supporting vehicles appeared to take part in the attack, only to come under withering fire from the German artillery.

"That's the crossroads," said a corporal, pointing across the fields with his sten-gun. "We must attack over the road to the left. That village in front is where the platoons are."

A sergeant pointed, "There's at least three battalions of Jerry holding the woods behind that road. Our task is to attack them with these tanks. They must be drawn away to save our platoons."

The order to fix bayonets rapped out, followed by the order to advance. Sick to their stomachs, the company moved into the open, into the teeth of the enemy's guns. Swiftly they forded the stream, doubled along the side of a hedgerow, shooting it up as they went in case of snipers and came to the open fields, still being swept by shellfire, and dropped flat on their faces.

Another platoon which was working on their flank had drawn level with them, so they moved forward together in file till they reached the roadside, where they again took cover. Here the smell of dead cattle was nauseating. Tanks and bren-carriers moved again. Up sprang the infantry like one man, and rushed across the road with a barrage from their own guns whistling over their heads. through woods and orchards they swept, all alive with snipers in varying degree of camouflage. On, on, they pressed, shooting up everything in front of them till, panting hard, they arrived at the far side of the trees.

It was here that the real enemy opposition was encountered ... A blistering hail of spandau fire met them as they slithered to a halt at the edge of a lane. Casualties mounted with frightening regularity. Other platoons, working on the flanks, were similarly held up. Mortars began to range on them.

The massive Weatherall did sterling work with his bren-gun, and by brute force ensured it was used to its maximum. Another move forward was attempted. Immediately a spandau opened up. The man in front of Weatherall dropped, his chest mangled with bullets. Weatherall pulled him to a fold in the ground, where he attempted first aid. It was useless; within minutes the man was dead.

Once again the company was pinned down, and unable to retaliate. To add to their problems, the setting sun silhouetted their figures into enormous black relief, much to the satisfaction of enemy marksmen. Eventually the order to withdraw was given. This they accomplished inch by inch, keeping their formation as they dodged from cover to cover. Suddenly a fearsome report, accompanied by severe blast, drove all except Weatherall earthwards. He, poor man, was propelled upwards, completed a somersault, and fell on his back at the foot of a tree. He was very shaken, and badly spattered with pieces of shrapnel. Several of his mates rushed to his aid. He could hardly move or speak, but still held valiantly to his bren-gun.

Between them the section managed to carry him across the road and set him on his back in a ditch. A few sips from a water-bottle worked wonders, and within minutes his sheer brawn was pulling him back to recovery. Finally he made it to a stretcher-bearer truck, which took him back to company headquarters. Here he was conveyed to a hospital near Bayeux, where he spent several weeks.

With the arrival in hospital of more and more of his company as casualties he was eventually able to build up a picture of what really happened during that terrible night.

It appeared that his whole company occupied the line of the road all night, despite the fact that the enemy retired at dusk, after firing a heavy barrage for some minutes to cover their retreat. Later some enemy patrols returned and made their presence felt, which kept the company from sleep. About 0130 hours the following morning tanks were heard approaching, and the company was about to engage them at point-blank range when it was discovered that they were the forward platoons of their own forces, coming out of the village they'd so gallantly held during the day. During the remainder of the night some enemy, either in groups or individually, did manage to filter through the battalion lines. From what Weatherall could gather there was no actual clear-cut fighting during all that time, only a general mix-up of friend and foe.

Meanwhile Morley and his company, the

'Spud-Patch' veterans, had not moved from their
position all that day, and only the same
bren-carrier as met up with Weatherall's company
gave them what little information there was
available. By evening Morley's company felt
confident that they wouldn't move again that
night and made preparations for sleep, only to be
told to make ready for an advance - on foot.

It was close to midnight when they moved
forward, Cragg's platoon in front. Their route
lay across country, to avoid the road, and this
made them feel even more isolated. They moved in
virtual silence, hugging the hedgerows and
ditches, alert for enemy snipers.

"Where are we going?" breathed Cragg to the
man next to him.

"Some crossroads or other, to take over from
the forward platoons," was the reply.

The nocturnal silence was more nervewracking
than any bombardment. Cragg looked at the sky;
it was largely clear of cloud, and pinpoints of
stars twinkled through. A glow lit the flank.
"Houses still burning from our attack." snorted a
sergeant.

Now in its last quarter, the moon hung over
their heads like a great moody balloon, as if it
too was confused by so much death and
destruction. Neither its light nor the light from
the fires was sufficient to reveal the ill-fated
bridge, screened as it was by trees from the gaze
of the men as they filed past within a few yards
of it. If they had been able to see it the story
might have been very different, for they would
surely have seen a daring group of Germans at
work on the bridge, laying mines and taking up
sniper positions. The chances are they would
have engaged and liquidated them, thus saving
so much trouble and death to their comrades later
on.

But it was not to be. Instead dawn found them
firmly entrenched around the crossroads,
unopposed, and ready for any eventuality.

At dawn the transport and supporting armoured
vehicles moved up to close with Morley's company.
They were spared the fierce shelling of the

previous day, for by now Jerry had retired. Their progress was unimpeded until they reached the bridge, where, under the impression it had been cleared of mines, they made preparations to cross. The only visible obstacle appeared to be a harmless cow's head, severed from its body by a shell, lying in the centre of the bridge.

Slowly the column moved across. The leading vehicle had just reached the bridge's arch when there was a shattering report, and a column of black smoke spiralled skywards. The echo of the explosion resounded across the dell and surrounding trees. The following vehicles ground to a halt.

"Mines." someone yelled.

"Impossible, the bridge was cleared yesterday," someone else shouted.

Several men rushed towards the stricken vehicle. One of its crew had been injured by the blast, while another had been blown onto the road and had crawled away.

"Where's the driver?" asked a rescuer.

"There, dead." one of the injured men pointed to a dust covered heap.

"Who is it?" an officer asked.

"Sawyer, sir."

A hurried consultation took place between the officers, while the column remained where it was. Engineers were called up to re-sweep and clear the bridge. Finally they were able to cross without further interruption. As reports filtered through it became evident that the bridge had been mined again during the hours of darkness by an enemy patrol, whom Morley and the rest of the company must just have missed seeing by the skin of their teeth. The cow's head had been the cover for their dastardly work.

The village and its crossroads were almost completely calm that day. The main topic of conversation was Sawyer's death, and many men expressed their deep regret, especially Grayson, who took pains to inform them of the incident of his being "mentioned in dispatches".

"If these past two weeks are a sample of what the rest of the war's going to be like, then there'll be none of us left," Copplestone said mournfully.

No one bothered to take him up on his statement, as all had succumbed to a heaviness of spirit well nigh intolerable.

Next day the sun had scarcely got up before a trail of dust from the direction of the bridge heralded the approach of a supply column. Within minutes a jeep pulled up at the crossroads and out jumped Calder. Magnetically, he drew his usual crowd.

"Great stuff lads, you've won." he said.

"Won what?" enquired several weary voices.

"The battle, of course - you've won, I tell you."

"Look, don't come here with any more stinking cookhouse rumours," snarled Copplestone with a rare burst of anger, as he turned away in disgust.

"Listen lads," Calder said gently. "I know how you're feeling. I know I promised you a trip to Paris and a place in the corps reserve, and they didn't come off. But this time it's true, and you'll know it before you're many minutes older."

"Get on with it, we're sick of your riddles." a burly sergeant said.

"O.K. then, the Yanks have got behind Jerry and he's caught in the ring. You've had a hard time capturing this place, but with the help of other units you managed to hold Jerry frontally while others made headway. That's why Jerry pulled out so suddenly the other night."

His words were too coincidental not to be true, and they knew it. Suddenly their attitude towards him changed. They bubbled with excitement, talked wildly, and jumped about as if released from prison - which in a manner of speaking they were.

"Fantastic, well done the Yanks - the war's over." they yelled.

These and a hundred other shouts rent the air. Then, as if the party was suddenly over, things went quiet. Obviously doubts still existed.

"Calder," said Vincent, looking really vicious, "if you're filling us full of boloney, I will personally kill you." He looked so menacing as his big hands clenched and unclenched that Calder took a step backwards.

But for once Calder had not lied. He had gleaned the truth. And to prove it the order came through to pack up and prepare to move - not forwards this time, but backwards. With the sun splitting the skies and warming the village and its crossroads that memorable Sunday morning, the whole battalion moved out, leaving the place to the care of another unit.

They moved to take up a tactical position a few miles to the rear. This was presumably intended to be a defensive position against an expected counter-attack, but this never happened, and the enemy was never again seen by the battalion in Normandy.

For on that very day the Germans began their historic retreat of the Falaise Gap.

Chapter Eleven

"Soldiering ain't what it used to be."

The voice came out of a group of squatting Tommies, gathered around a small petrol-cooker on which was perched a dixie, almost brim-full of water on the point of boiling.

"It's not even what it was when we were in Yorkshire," the voice went on sadly. "I don't know where it's going to end. All I've done for the past three weeks is load and unload ammo, tons of it."

"Darn good job you didn't have to be on the receiving end of it like poor old Jerry, Phelps," Rattray said.

Having cracked his 'funny' Rattray poured a liberal handful of a mixture of tea, milk, and sugar onto the water, allowed it to boil, then removed the dixie from the cooker, placed it on the ground, and skimmed off some of the floating mass. He went on to fill the neat line of waiting mugs, which were quickly claimed by their owners.

"I'm very glad we don't have a trip to the line to-night, what do you say Henshaw?"

"No I'm not glad; I'm all for it," Henshaw said, draining his mug. "They seem to think just because we're 'on supply' we've been having an easy time, because we haven't been up forward. Let's face it, it's been just as bad in other ways."

This was the truth, and anyone who knew anything about the lot of lorry-drivers of Normandy during this period would have agreed. For during their day and night trips to the front line with supplies they endured untold miseries from dust and danger, and were all suffering from a considerable lack of sleep, so much so that they finally got beyond the need for it.

That night they had their longest sleep in three weeks, and by the third successive night of comparatively peaceful slumber, were beginning to show signs of revival.

Situated as they were in a large field, Phelps and Rattray did their best to entertain around the dixie. As often as not this took the form of arguments and discussions about every subject under the sun, including 'when I get back to civvy street....'

One day, during one of these interminable discussions, Cragg and Catley rolled up. This turned into a massively lengthy meeting, during which the dixie did yeoman service. There was an awful lot of catching up to be done. Everyone swapped yarns, suitably coloured, but none had quite the same effectiveness as those told by the two 'Spud Patch' men. Later, some of the others paid 'official visits', including Henshaw, Cunningham and Grayson. Sawyer's death and Weatherall's injury were the subjects of lengthy conversation. Regarding Thorpe, they could only surmise where he was or what might have happened to him.

In the event, it so happened that he was only several miles to the north of them, 'holed-up' in a similar field to their own, and with no more facilities or comforts. For the most part his thoughts turned in a southernly direction, towards his mates, or at least to where he considered they might be. His part in the Normandy operation had been unspectacular, driving around in a jeep well behind the firing-line. However he did have one close shave on the ridge near Caen, when enemy bombers paid one of their nightly visits. But since then nothing had happened to mar the calmness of his daily routine. Apart from a brief encounter with Calder, he had no definite information about the safety of his comrades, though he continued to enquire from all whom he met as to their welfare, and it was only through this inquisitiveness that he heard of Sawyer's death and Weatherall's mishap.

Thorpe considered himself lucky. His friends had been constantly in the front line, while he had been kept well to the rear. He had no overwhelming desire to change places with them, for his taste for front-line fighting was of the limited variety. Nonetheless he was with his friends in spirit, for he was not the kind of man to allow others, particularly friends, to pass through unpleasant experiences from which he himself had been spared without acknowledging his debt to them.

His eyes fell upon a Cross of Calvary, just across the road from his position. It was a common sight in Normandy, and he felt that its presence was particularly relevant to the bitter fighting they were all engaged in. His gaze then fell on a burnt-out farmhouse, around which a family had gathered with some pitifully few livestock and several barrow-loads of belongings – all that had survived the onslaught. He prayed that the sacrifice of the inhabitants of Normandy would not be in vain, and would never be forgotten.

His mind formed a neat precis of the whole horrible carnage they were involved in – it was that one man, the Son of God, had died for all men, to save them for the next world, and since that time it was given to some men to die for others, to preserve them by fighting in this world.....

All too quickly the division's rest period drew to a close. Of all the events which happened about that time, one deserves special mention. That was the promotion of Calder, which was announced quite suddenly one afternoon, to the amusement of some and the disgust of others.

"So you're taking the tapes then?" sneered Copplestone. "How do you think you'll get on with a section?"

"Why, in the usual way, ninety per-cent bluff." said Calder.

This raised a howl of approval.

"Well, I suppose it's something to reach the dizzy heights of Lance Corporal, but in one way it's the lowest form of life. You get precious little thanks from the sergeants and you're not popular with the privates," Vincent said charmingly.

Undeterred, Calder grinned, "The only thing that's worrying me about the whole affair is being parted from this old girl." He patted his jeep fondly.

"I wish I'd known, there was a Yank around the other day attempting to swap one for a Jerry pistol." some wag said.

But the dye was cast for Calder, and within days he'd moved to higher things in another platoon.

Some days later the battalion was ordered to a new concentration area. The sun split the skies on the day they moved. On the way they passed the village and the crossroads, which they now saw in a very different light. The new rendezvous, though pleasant enough, was not intended to be their home for very long, for almost immediately rumours of a lengthy advance to the fighting areas began to circulate. However, they did wait long enough for reinforcements to arrive. One of these, with his familiar laugh and unquenchable tongue, turned out to be none other than Crabtree, just returned from England. Another person who joined them at that time was Hilton. It appeared he'd been sent back to a reinforcement camp somewhere to the rear, and had only now been called forward.

The newcomers were soon up-dated with the facts about the Normandy Campaign in general and with the exploits of the 'Spud Patch' company in particular. Amidst the jokes and laughter Morley thought fit to inject a serious note to the effect that by now all the 'front line' men knew what it was like to be thoroughly scared, and that it was no shame to see brave men cry, especially when in the end their sense of duty would always prevail.

The arrival of the reinforcements was in itself an indication of an early move. Extra petrol and rations were issued, accompanied by the usual briefing of officers and N.C.O's. The whole battalion was lined up in order of march, and soon afterwards it pulled out onto the road. It was a quarter to five on a Monday afternoon, and it augured the beginning of what was destined to be the most thrilling week of their lives.

However, it started off normally enough as they crawled slowly along the road and passed through a fair sized town. They turned left and headed north-east at a steady speed, which lasted till nightfall when it dropped to half-speed. It felt good to be able to coast along without the dreaded fear of being sniped at. In the light of the new moon the countryside slept. In this fashion they kept to the main road, every now and again passing through a burnt out village. After a time the woods grew thinner till eventually they petered out altogether, to be replaced by large open spaces. These spaces were open but far from empty. First the hulk of a burnt out tank loomed large in the night sky, then a dozen others became silhouetted in a group; then in quick succession, scores of guns, tanks, and tracked vehicles, all still and ghostlike as the moon lit up their fire-scorched frames. This scene was repeated for several miles and included hundreds upon hundreds of vehicles, all in the same state.

Copplestone, who until then had been enjoying a snooze in the back of his truck, suddenly jerked bolt upright at the sight of these monsters from another age.

"What are they?" he gasped, his mind attempting to translate what his eyes saw.

"A bunch of violets." Vincent said sarcastically.

"They're Jerry, all of them. This must be The Gap, the Argentan-Falaise Gap we've all been hearing so much about," said Morley, as usual the fountain of all knowledge.

An N.C.O. chipped in, "This is what happened to him when he started his retreat the night after the attack on the crossroads. Our Typhoons bombed him from the air, and what was left the Yanks and our own units up this end finished off."

"And we thought it was rough where we were. It was a flea-bite compared to what Jerry copped," Morley said.

"True," said Copplestone. He sank back into his truck. He'd seen quite enough of the devastation to last him for a very long time.

The column diverted onto a detour, and because of the chaos still ahead, the men saw no more. The moon disappeared behind a cloud, and the next few hours were spent in see-sawing first down one side road, then back up another, dodging demolitions, road-blocks and shattered villages in the process. Once again, due to the volume of traffic, the already poor state of the roads rapidly became worse, and this was not helped by a rainstorm which turned the track into a quagmire. Despite this they kept going, and did not harbour till just before dawn. Here they were to spend the next twenty-four hours in hastily prepared bowers in wheatfields, or under dripping trees.

On the move again, the scenery changed for the better as they travelled through picturesque countryside, and towns where civilians moved about freely and waved to them, even occasionally raising a cheer. As other units had preceded them, the local population were by now becoming used to the sight of Tommy.

The further north they travelled, the less became the signs of war, and the green of the fields deepened. Cautiously they allowed their spirits to rise. Here, at least for the moment, there was peace.

It was midday before they once again encountered the familiar and unpleasant sight of a battlefield, and that peculiar smell which hung over everything. They had reached a bombed out area close to the Seine. Instantly they dropped their speed to a crawl. As they wound their way through a town they caught several glimpses of the river through gaps in the buildings, as it swirled its way towards the sea. A pontoon bridge had been thrown across, and within minutes they were on the other side and roaring up a slope, and into some thick woods which opened onto cornfields at the summit of the hill, overlooking the river. Here they deployed and halted.

"Two hours rest," came the rapid order.

They had a mere two hours to refuel and cook some food. Soon they were fed with another piece of information. "Amiens, the immediate objective; final objective, Brussels." Surely someone was talking nonsense. It would take weeks to reach either of these at the pace they'd moved through Normandy. 'Amiens, Brussels'... just names on a map – miles away. The respite came to an end, and they moved onwards.

What did the future hold for them?

Chapter Twelve

Cragg's platoon was leading, and Hilton was driving the third vehicle. He tried to catch a glimpse of a map which the N.C.O. by his side was flirting with, on which their route was marked. He made out a circle with an arrow pointing to it; this represented the night's resting-place. It all seemed incredibly far from the Seine; it must be a mistake.

They bounced over fields and onto the road, the surface of which had several inches of soft, slippery mud, churned up by preceding convoys. Their speed quickened, for they had orders to 'get up front'. Soon it developed into one mad rush, the survival of the fittest, and for the next few hours Hilton and every other driver in front or behind whirled in and out of the accompanying convoys, missing them by inches, and only escaping driving into ditches or rolling down banks by a hairs-breadth -- but never for a moment slackening speed. Tanks were also included in this mad-cap race, and when the road became too narrow the tanks took to the fields, and churned them into mud pools in their frenzy. Not until the rival column had been left well behind did they slacken speed, and then only for an instant.

"We're still not in front," snapped the N.C.O. beside Hilton.

The vehicle in front careered forward, and Hilton followed. They soon reached top speed again. Through towns and villages they tore, each one jammed with crowds, all cheering fit to burst at the recollection of their recent liberation.

Shaven-headed women were being paraded through the streets and jeered at in retaliation for collaboration with the enemy. In the countryside both men and women helped themselves to the abandoned equipment of the departing Germans. But the British had no time to halt for any of these things, and had to content themselves with a cursory wave at the crowds as they sped through the soft green countryside. They covered practically forty miles before they met up with the leading unit, and then only because the latter had been halted by a pocket of enemy infantry. It appeared that this delay would be a lengthy one, so they were ordered to move off the road and deploy. Dusk fell with them still stationary, so they set to and prepared a meal. A reconnaissance unit pulled in close by, presumably with the idea of harbouring for the night, and with no specific orders to the contrary the various companies and squadrons involved assumed they were in for a night's rest.

However it was not to be, for shortly after midnight they got the dreaded order 'prepare to move'. The splutter of starting engines broke the stillness of the night, and the air became filled with curses and moans. It was sheer madness to advance at that hour. What on earth could the destination possibly be? Doubtless they were aware that everything would become clear in the fullness of time, but for the moment they were, to a man, in a foul temper.

They had only just started to achieve some momentum, when they were halted.

"What now?" growled Grayson, as he heard an officer's voice say "We're just about level with them now."

"Level with whom; the enemy pocket?" Grayson quizzed himself. He didn't know, and no one enlightened him.

Whether it was the enemy pocket or not, nothing happened, and Grayson, who'd been displaced from his usual position behind Crabtree by another truck, saw the column move to the left, with the exception of the truck which had displaced him. This vehicle continued to remain stationary for some time, while Grayson fumed behind. Finally, his patience exhausted, he approached on foot and yanked open the driver's door – he had fallen asleep.

"Wake up; the column's gone on." Grayson thundered.

"What, gone on?" befuddled with sleep, the driver's reactions were slow.

"Get moving, they've gone left," Grayson shouted, diving for his truck.

Their luck was in, for a few hundred yards

down the road they made contact with the others. Progress became painfully slow as thick woods closed them in on both sides, and the sheer blackness of the night resembled a tunnel. The crimson tail-lights of each vehicle, swaying up and down like ships in a high sea, alone pierced the night, and acted as a welcome guide to the following vehicle. Grayson's eyes grew dizzy with the strain of keeping them on the tail-light in front, and the fight to keep awake became all consuming. How many pockets of enemy, how many snipers' eyes observed them from the cover of trees, they would never know; but they made it without incident.

At a halt shortly before dawn, Grayson felt sleep overpowering him. In the gloom he saw a figure standing close to his vehicle. His confused brain immediately thought it was a German; he gasped with fear, and the figure moved. Then others appeared, and surprised voices began talking, "Les Anglais."

He sank into his seat with relief. It was a newly liberated French village, and his company was the first British unit to pass through. At first light they were rolling into the village, already awake and preparing to receive them. The welcome was in French, so only a limited number were able to understand, but a girl who had some knowledge of English placed herself at the line of the convoy and with the aid of a white handkerchief, which she kept raising and lowering, said as each vehicle passed, "Well done boys; welcome." During the brief moment of a halt someone thrust an egg into Grayson's hand. It was the first he'd seen for weeks, and seemed to him more than fair recompense for a sleepless night.

The sun shone, their speed increased, suddenly as the road dipped they saw the town of Beauvais a short distance in front. The crackle of small-arms fire followed by the sight of a dozen or so Germans, hands above their heads, rushing out to surrender, caused another halt. Finally they entered the town. It was wide awake and with the sound of firing still very much in evidence, all pockets of resistance were soon cleared up. Soon the natural French hospitality exerted itself, and the troops were overwhelmed with invitations to drink coffee and wine. Picking up information as best they could from their hosts of the moment, the column learnt that the Germans had left the town the previous evening, riding on bicycles or anything else they could commandeer. Earlier, Jerry had machine-gunned the streets as a farewell blessing.

Afterwards Grayson handed over to his relief driver, and, exhausted, sank down in the mate's seat in the hope of sleeping a little. But it was hopeless, the break-neck speed they were forced to maintain made it impossible. Through village after village they roared, receiving a tremendous welcome in each. Copplestone and Vincent, who were in the rear of Grayson's vehicle, made so much noise shouting to the crowds that eventually Grayson abandoned all thoughts of sleep and took over the wheel again.

The morning was perfect, and the fields and woods, bathed in sunlight, were havens of peace. Several light tanks could be seen reconnoitring to the right, but nothing else was visible. The long, snake-like British column stretched for miles to the rear. At a dip in the road an ominous crackling sound put nerves on edge, but it turned out to be nothing more than a German half-track armoured truck on fire; it had been set alight by its crew after they had been unable to obtain any further fuel. The crew surrendered without resistance, but this had the effect of forcing the whole column off the road for a while to dodge the exploding ammunition.

With the vortex of events everyone's spirits began to rise. Even the usually sombre Morley began to feel at peace with the world as he sat on the seat beside Vincent, puffing hard on his pipe. Within view was Hilton's truck, with Cragg posted by its Browning, while Oatley's vehicle was a few yards behind his own. Slightly further back he saw L/Corporal Calder laughing, at ease in the middle of his section. Spottiswoode and Crabtree were in their usual places, and each vehicle was by now well supplied with rations – all in all Morley felt that not much more could be desired.

The leading tanks started to deploy at the edge of a wood while the remainder of the column edged slowly forward; all eyes were glued on the progress of the tanks. As they moved past the wood unchallenged everyone breathed a sigh of relief; the enemy had vacated it. But instead of Germans, out of the wood from behind numerous clumps of trees emerged a number of gaunt, unshaven figures.

"Must be the Maquis," an N.C.O. said.

"Well armed too, you'd wonder how they got those weapons. Must have picked them up from an R.A.F. drop," said Morley.

The weary Maquis, after smiling at the troops, filed on down the road to disappear over the skyline, their task completed.

A troop of recce cars overtook the company and passed to the front.

"We must have been in front of the recce boys last night. Glad I wasn't in the front tank," Grayson said.

With the arrival of the reconnaissance troop their speed increased noticeably. When an hour had passed with only a German horse-drawn vehicle, already shot up and looted by the Maquis, in evidence, it began to dawn on the men that the enemy was actually in flight.

"It looks as if we'll make Amiens quicker than we thought," a corporal said.

As in all campaigns, only a favoured few knew the actual position of the column at any given time, or where the objectives were. To the ordinary soldier all was unknown, and he became so programmed to this state of affairs that it never occurred to him to ask for details.

Now, however, this was one observation that he needed no instruction in–the fact that the enemy was on the run. So different from the Normandy Campaign, where every yard of ground had been fiercely contested. Now, in line ahead, the armoured column were motoring on virtually unmolested. No wonder there was a terrific surge

95

of pent-up feeling, which bore every man along, and surmounted all hunger pangs or lack of sleep effects.

"Wish they would keep us going, now we've really started. I could keep going to Berlin," Morley said, clenching his teeth.

About midday a large town came into view. A light breeze wafted the sound of firing from somewhere behind it. In excellent order, proceeding slowly, the column approached it. Everyone was prepared for another fight, but the Maquis were almost entirely in possession, and as the streets resounded with the squealing tracks of the British tanks the townsfolk, like rats from a sinking ship, came out of their hiding places to welcome them. Inevitably a major traffic jam was created for a time, and this signalled a halt while another company took up position in front. Excited civilians clambered all over tanks, cigarettes were passed around, and the majority attempted to converse in a mixture of French and English, each side making the maximum use of suitable gestures.

Morley and Copplestone took advantage of the proceedings to cook breakfast, and this included Grayson's egg which had been presented to him at Beauvais. A number of French housewives monitored these preparations, and were fascinated by the method of coping with the stew, bully-beef and biscuits, all in the one mess-tin. The demonstration was badly interrupted by the splutter of a bren-gun close by. This sent everyone diving for cover.

"Jerry tank," shouted the bren-gunner.

He'd noticed the tank arrive at a crossroads barely a hundred yards away. On halting, several of its crew jumped out, hit the road, and stood looking about, obviously unaware of the presence of British troops. With a considerable show of initiative the bren-gunner boldly engaged them, firing his gun from the shoulder and hoping to force them to surrender. Instead, the driver, who'd remained inside the tank, on hearing the burst of fire turned his vehicle and made off, leaving his hapless comrades to face the British. They surrendered without further struggle, and were only spared severe punishment from the Maquis by the keen-eyed British guards.

"Is this Amiens?" asked Vincent.

"No, Villiers Bretonneux; I've just been told," said Copplestone.

"That name's familiar, I'm sure my uncle mentioned it in connection with the last war," said Vincent.

"Quite right," said Grayson, who'd been conversing with one of the Maquis in English. "He says he remembers the British here in 1918."

It was several hours before the company moved again, and when they did they noticed much evidence of First World War activities, including several cemeteries and a memorial column, all well kept, which lay in their path. But there was little opportunity to inspect these as they were ordered to advance at full speed down the valley, on account of enemy anti-tank guns which had begun to range on the road. Several enemy snipers made things uncomfortable before they got underway, but finally every vehicle moved off at top speed down the hill, each crew keeping his head well down and hanging on grimly.

The valley seemed bottomless, and the few minutes required to dash through it seemed like an hour. But they made it and eventually, one by one, they bumped across the bridge over the Aire river, obstacle of World War One, and into a small town. The main street was packed with halted vehicles, and civilians milled about everywhere.

The bridge had been captured intact, but the leading tanks, on emerging from the far end of the town had fallen foul of the hidden enemy anti-tank guns. It would have been suicide for the others to have proceeded, so the whole column was forced to take a detour to the left.

"Jerry allowed the recce to get through, and then let the tanks have it," muttered a corporal, quoting information received from someone nearer the front of the column.

"He knows his stuff, he's still able to play his cards well," laughed Copplestone.

97

Tricolours began to appear from the houses, like mushrooms in a field on a dewy morning.

"Is it safe to hang these out yet, Monsieur?" a French civilian enquired of Vincent, who prescribed patience for a little longer.

The detour was across fields, and involved several large woods which had to be cleared. For an hour the drivers stood guard over their vehicles, which were down in the hollow in range of some uncomfortable sniper fire. Many trenches, preserved intact from the previous war, ran through the hollow in snake-like formation.

"Look at these, to think men occupied them for months, even years." said Grayson in amazement.

"While here we are to-day, driving along hour after hour with hardly a stop," croaked Spottiswoode, as a bullet pinged over his head and lodged in a tree.

The woods were cleared and the whole battalion, together with the tank squadrons, advanced a mile or so to higher ground where they harboured for the night. Dusk fell, with once again the sound of picks and shovels hacking the earth, and the background noise of mess-tins and cooking utensils.

It had been a day of achievement, with no casualties, and over eighty miles covered inside twenty four hours, and with Amiens by-passed and behind them.

Groups of Maquis patrolled the area, and their watchfulness was tested with the appearance of a car bearing a red-cross, travelling at speed. Aware that this was Jerry on reconnaissance they opened up with a fusillade of shots, but the vehicle survived, and the occupants lost little time in returning whence they came, doubtless with a suitably coloured account of enemy oppositional strengths.

Next morning at first light the chase was on again, with this time the main body of the battle-group playing a supporting role to another part of the division. Morley's company was tasked to sort out an enemy pocket, before it could join in the liberating run.

A sergeant informed them that Jerry was

holding a place several miles up the road, and they had to see that he didn't get out. It was useless moaning, for the job had to be done. Already the platoons were lined up in order, awaiting the word to move. Within minutes they were gliding out of the harbouring area and down the road to the north.

It was a pale grey morning, and the only sound came from the vehicle tracks as they lumbered across gentle slopes. A small fire down in the valley of the Aire was the only diversion. The road ran straight for some distance, which made the going easy to start with, but a fold in the ground soon drastically reduced their speed. On the far side an enemy bazooka team was engaged by the leading tank before they could range on it. After one of their number was wounded the others were only too eager to surrender.

Isolated shots rang out from distant slopes, and Oatley's section was tasked to investigate, while the rest negotiated the long, gentle rise.

"Be careful, those slopes are alive with Jerry," a soldier from the reconnaissance unit said. "They've already fired on us, so we let them have it."

Oatley's section could be seen picking up one of the victims.

"Keep off the skyline," ordered a voice over the radio. "There are eighty-eights in the town."

Obediently the tanks lumbered off the road and fanned out into the fields. The platoons on the road now braved the crest, and began the descent into what looked like a small town. On the way more First War trenches were observed, and every half mile a raised parapet jutted out from a field.

"We're living history all over again. Just imagine men actually walking up and down these to the line. They could tell a story," Morley said.

By the time their section was over the crest the leading platoon had reached the outskirts of the town, and the order to de-bus was given. The drivers only remained behind, while the rest hurried forward on foot. Their mortars opened up with covering fire, and the company entered

unchallenged; but not for long. Spandau fire from
the houses soon made things uncomfortable for the
attackers, and the forward platoon was caught
crossing the road. It became difficult to return
fire as the machine-gun nests were invisible from
the road. Several sections scrambled over a
railway line, only to find themselves exposed to
a merciless small-arms fire from other enemy
positions. Men began to drop, and a tank was hit.

Undaunted, the company tried every possible
means to push forward, but each time they found
their way blocked. The place was obviously very
strongly held, and to persist with the attack
would have been costly and purposeless. The only
viable alternative was to attempt to contain the
Germans, so an order to withdraw to the high
ground was given. This proved to be as perilous
as the attack itself, especially to the men on the
other side of the railway-line, who didn't dare
lift their heads above the scanty cover.

Finally an N.C.O. took the initiative, and
using a two inch mortar sent a couple of
explosive and smoke bombs in the direction of the
enemy. The smoke screen lasted just long enough
for the men to spring across the railway line and
join their comrades, who'd started to move back.

Once back in the trucks the company regained
the crest, behind which they dug in, with the
object of denying the enemy any chance of using
the road for a counter attack against the main
line of the British advance. With the rest of the
division now miles ahead, the company was left
on its own. The Germans made no further attempt
to molest them, and tediously the day wore on.
Civilians moved in and out of the town quite
unconcernedly. Towards evening everyone was
startled by the appearance of a British scout-car
which tore down the road from the direction of
the town. After a good deal of waving and
shouting from the company, it was brought to a
halt.

One of the crew said, "We've come from Arras.
We came from the other side in the hope that
you'd captured the town. But we soon discovered
that you hadn't. We gave Jerry a burst and

100

cleared out." He laughed nervously.

This was the climax of the day. At 2000 hours several infantry units appeared and put in an attack on the town. The company, relieved of its charge, returned to the same harbouring area it had left that morning.

Next day they pressed on for Arras, and reached it in three hours, hectic driving. Despite their lateness they were cheered loudly as they shot through to take their place in the battle-group. The rest of the day was spent in the repair and maintenance of vehicles, which had suffered almost as rough a time as the men in them. The rest of the evening was their own, and the men made strenuous efforts to relax, but the operational cycle of the front-line soldier was such that rest hovered between partial or not at all. Orders continued to be issued in which there appeared to be two alternative plans for the next day. One mentioned the dropping of paratroopers along the line of advance, in which case reveille would not be till 0700 hours. The other, more negative in content, stated that if the airborne operation was cancelled, reveille would be at 0500 hours.

"Apparently it all hinges on the weather," said Crabtree knowingly. "If it is unsuitable for paratroopers we move early."

"Well, when will we know if it is suitable or not? How am I supposed to rest if I con't know what time we must move?" someone groaned.

"No news is good news. They'd have told us before this if we were moving early," said Vincent optimistically.

"Hope you're right." said Copplestone, flinging himself onto his bed....

****

The negative plan won the day. The airborne operation was cancelled, and reveille was at 0500 hours.

At 0600 hours the battalion was once again streaming down the road northwards, this time towards the sound of gunfire. Soon they halted, and once again a returning stretcher-bearer truck became the sign that the leading company had already engaged the enemy.

"Enemy pocket ahead. S.S. Troops," yelled the driver as he drove on.

The pocket proved to be a tough one, and after considerable delay a company with tanks - Weatherall's company less Weatherall of course - was detailed to remain to cope with it. The remainder of the battle-group branched to the right and took a detour through villages and roads, lined with cheering people.

"That must be Lens," said Grayson, viewing the slag heaps common to mining country. Familiar First War names continued to appear on sign-posts, which shot by in increasing numbers, the pace was becoming so hectic.

"Look at those pill-boxes." yelled Morley. "That's the Gort line we manned way back in nineteen thirty nine. Never thought we'd see those again."

In a village the column halted momentarily.

"Vive la France," shouted Grayson at a group of people.

"C'est Belge ici," they shouted back.

"Boy oh boy, we're in Belgium already," gasped Morley, who was so overcome at seeing old sights that he was finding it difficult to remain in his seat.

Onwards and ever faster they moved, through towns and villages with unpronounceable Belgian names. Past stately churches, over bridges, across canals and along cobbled roads thundered the British column, always to the accompaniment of wild bursts of cheering from the civilian population. Tournai was reached, and left behind. The speed became madder, engines were in danger of overheating. Surely the tanks would never be able to stick it?

But stick it they did as mile after mile was eaten up. At every village and crossroads the locals gathered, including priests in their flat black hats and gowns all cheering like schoolboys. Flowers and fruit showered down onto tanks and trucks as each community endeavoured to show its gratitude. Tiny children, born under the Hitler regime, stood giving the Nazi salute, for they knew no other. Across fields and fences, old men and women, boys and girls, all dressed in their Sunday best, raced to cheer and shout, often arriving at the road too late, as the column in its frantic rush had already passed, leaving them to weep gently or wave madly at those still to come.

"We're halting," said Morley suddenly.

"Tanks refuelling. Looks as if we'll go on without them," a corporal said.

Someone passed word back that they were twenty miles behind the other spearhead of the division, which was advancing on another road. Ahead they saw about a hundred Germans at the side of the road, all with their hands up in surrender while several bren-carriers kept them covered.

"First sign of Jerry to-day, apart from that first pocket. How far have we come?" Morley asked.

Grayson checked his mileometer. "Fifty two miles," he said.

They remained stationary for some minutes to allow the tanks to catch up, when they all proceeded with a further spurt which took them to a large town. This like all the others was bedecked with flowers and flags and jammed with people, all wanting to welcome the conquerors. A number of Germans came through the town, being escorted, and the crowd indulged in a good deal of booing.

"Tough looking merchants," said Vincent, as one glared defiantly at him." They look thrashed though."

Out of the town the column tore at breakneck speed.

"They say we'll be in Brussels to-night," an N.C.O. said.

On, ever onwards they moved, bouncing along the cobbled roads, around detours, past dozens of groups of elated Belgians.

"I never thought this truck could go so fast," Cragg yelled above the roar of the engine.

"I've flogged it to death and it still keeps going," said Hilton.

As they approached yet another village Cragg shouted, "Keep your foot on that accelerator; another shower of apples from the crowd will just about finish us. We've more apples than bullets aboard as it is."

They passed houses, crowds and flags, the way a through train does at a station.

"How did we do?" asked Hilton.

"Only landed two this time." shouted Cragg. "But keep up with the column, they're going flat out."

"They call this 'swanning'," said Cragg after a while. "It's a new kind of war, you just keep going. Of course it all depends on the enemy being kind enough to let you."

"Just too bad for those who break-down. There must be many Jerry pockets just waiting the chance to pounce on a single truck," someone said.

"Several have already dropped out; not many, but we've been lucky so far," Cragg said.

"Something's happening up front," said Hilton, as he peered through the vizor of his truck.

"We're pulling to the side of the road. Oh, I see, look out. Lightnings, Yankee Lightnings."

"Get the flares quick, or they'll have us." an N.C.O. ordered.

In an instant yellow smoke flares were hurled onto the road and immediately began to emit their reassuring screen of safety. The Lightnings sheered away, their pilots apparently satisfied that the column was Allied.

"Guess we gave them a shock too," said Cragg as he watched them disappear at dizzy speed. "Probably never expected us to be so far ahead."

Further on the column came to a dead stop in a lane somewhere along another detour from the main road, one of the many detours they'd experienced that day, presumably to dodge pockets of enemy or minefields.

"There's Brussels." several voices yelled simultaneously. In the soft evening light the great city stood silhouetted clearly. There could be no mistaking where it was.

"There's several fires burning," said Hilton.

"Reckon it's Jerry at work," said Cragg.

An uncomfortable few minutes passed, made more so by sniper fire from the direction of the cornfields. However, this enemy pocket surrendered easily enough when an N.C.O. approached and fired a burst of sten over their heads. About a dozen enemy revealed themselves, with their hands up, but due to the speed of the column there was no means of holding them, so they were sent down to be handed over to the tender mercy of the Belgian underground in the next village.

2000 hours found the column on the main road again. Radio messages received indicated that they were to enter the city.

"What, not into Brussels to-night? It's madness to attack a city of this size at night," Morley spluttered.

"What's to stop us harbouring here till morning?" growled Vincent. "What's the opposition anyway, has anyone a clue?"

"The usual enemy pocket plus some eighty-eights," sniggered a radio operator.

"So that's our lot then," muttered Grayson, sighing heavily and slamming the armour plating of his vehicle. He said a quick prayer to himself, appropriate for much a moment as everyone was exhausted after the dash and in no fit state, either physically or mentally, to attack a city the size of Brussels. The splutter of the machine-gun on the leading tank put them on the alert. Two German motor-cyclists, the recipients of the burst, had actually run head-on into the British without realising they had arrived. This indicated the degree of chaos which existed among the enemy still holding positions in the city.

All guns were ready for immediate use as the column moved forward, but none was required. Instead of the enemy confronting them in fierce hand-to-hand fighting, at every street corner the British soldiers were halted by a hilarious crowd of Bruxellois, who spilled out from houses and hiding places in their best Sunday clothes, cheering madly, waving flags and handkerchieves and throwing hats and belongings high into the air in gay abandon. The column proceeded steadily to the centre of the city, where the crowd increased so that it seemed every square inch of space was taken up. How the troops managed to drive through without knocking down any of that surging, struggling mass of humanity, none of the drivers ever knew.

Down street after street they tore, following one after another with the greatest difficulty. Had a German fired at them they would have been powerless to retaliate. At full speed they swept past the Palais de Justice, whose towers still glowed with fire, the result of German incendiary work, then shot through the narrow space which divided the milling crowd, packed tighter and tighter the closer they got to the city centre. Dodging through several hundred zealots, busy burning Nazi belongings outside the palace, without slackening speed, they arrived at the very heart of the city.

Even here there was no time to stop, and the excited Bruxellois had to expend their ardour on the troops which followed, whose vehicles soon became like mobile Kew Gardens, with swarms of individuals attempting to hug and kiss them.

A further mile, and the company's objective for the night was reached. It turned out to be a bridge, not mined, thanks to the efforts of the Belgian White Brigade. They crossed and slowed down on the bank of a canal and fanned out to occupy defensive positions in case of counter-attack. But the halt was fatal, for no sooner had word got around that there were British troops in the area than out of houses, cellars and buildings rushed the locals, like a swarm of locusts, without regard for personal danger. They surrounded the Tommies and hugged, kissed, danced with them. To the emotional people of Brussels the metamorphosis from German to Allied occupation, all done in the space of an hour, was all too much. Now the city only wanted to play. Lights burned everywhere, trams clanked backwards and forwards between the British and what remained of the enemy lines. Wine flowed like water. All this tended to drown the shots still issuing from back streets, where the Belgians were giving back what they owed Jerry who was still holed up in hiding places.

English, French and Flemish tongues all wagged hard; cigarettes were passed around, and liberators and liberated felt as if they'd known each other for a lifetime. Now and again a tremendous flash lit up the sky, always accompanied by wild cheering from the crowd, as yet another German ammunition dump was disposed of. Sleep for the populace was not a consideration that night. To them the war was over, and the presence of the British was a cause for unrestrained celebration. Tommy was expected to join in, otherwise it would not have been complete. How many invitations to houses were refused that night the lads never knew; all were genuine, and how difficult it was to decline them courteously. As fast as one group of eager people were put off, others pressed forward even more warmly. There could be no denying that the efforts to show gratitude were unique.

"They must think we're heroes," whispered Vincent to Morley, after each had refused a score of invitations.

"Must do, and us only humble British soldiers," the latter replied.

An extraordinarily tall man could be seen pushing his way through the crowd towards them.

"I know where eight hundred Germans are to be found," he declared in excellent English. "Shall I take you to them? They're only six hundred yards away."

"How far?" bawled Morley.

"Six hundred yards away, in barges," was the reply.

"Not on your life," hissed Morley, looking around for cover. "Eight hundred of them, and here we are standing like idiots talking to this giddy bunch of people. Has someone reported it?"

But no one could get to the bottom of that particular rumour, and Morley certainly wasn't going to find out single-handed. Whether true or not, the enemy was not bothering them. It was obvious Jerry had only one thought that night, and that was to get away as fast as possible, by road or canal or whatever way he could.

"Some victory," said Vincent, as dawn broke over the unresting city.

"Not a shot fired by us, except at those two motor-cyclists," Grayson said.

But 'les femmes jolies' had perhaps the best time of all, as they turned out to tempt the vulnerable Tommies with looks and words and the help of wine; which in the nature of things turned into many an orgy. Small thanks in a way for their fair city being spared a great destruction...

Chapter Thirteen

But Brussels did not lack patriots. The White Brigade, or underground movement, whose determined efforts had done so much to ensure that the British made such a triumphant entry into the city, continued its work at dawn.

All remaining civilian vehicles in the city were commandeered by these brave men in their ruthless search for the enemy. While they drove and hunted, their comrades cheered. The British had little to do, for these men were in complete control of the situation and knew any likely enemy hide-outs much better than any Allied army could have done.

Shortly after sunrise the remainder of the division entered Brussels. With it came Thorpe in his jeep, seeming to be singled out for special attention by the crowd. He was literally mobbed, and it wasn't long before his vehicle was packed with Bruxellois of both sexes, cascading him with garlands of flowers. One would have thought that he was the divisional commander who single-handed had masterminded the release of the city.

A re-run of the previous evening's activities was enacted as the latest arrivals moved through the street. At one point Thorpe passed close to some stationary vehicles, and thought he recognised Henshaw and Cunningham, but the throng was so intense that he was unable to make contact. He was right, it was Henshaw's outfit, and they were making the best of their stay in Brussels. Rattray had passed on the information that they would be there for at least four days, so they made themselves as comfortable as possible and prepared to 'mash down' despite the excited populace which surged around them.

"Did you know we'd created a record yesterday?" said Rattray.

"What sort of a record?" asked Henshaw.

"We covered almost a hundred miles; that's a record advance for one day for any division, if you're interested."

"There's no doubt we covered some ground, I

never thought when we crossed the Seine that we'd be in Brussels the same week." said Cunningham.

They'd just finished their meal when some ominous activity from the other companies indicated a move. They gleaned that they were to move to Louvain within the hour.

"I knew four days was too good to be true," sulked Phelps.

In a short while they'd left the city. The fifteen miles to Louvain were covered without trouble, and once again the column entered this famous university town to the familiar roar of welcome from its inhabitants. There was little resistance left. A small number of snipers kept up some intermittent firing until the British retaliated with incendiary bullets, setting the houses they occupied on fire. As with Brussels, the main problem was how to cope with the crowds, whose one desire was to entertain the liberators. The throng included a number of priests who, dressed in their long black frock coats and large brimmed hats, or brown loose garments and bare legs, represented a fair proportion of the gathering.

"We are delighted you have come so soon," said a tall bearded priest, approaching the section. This remark had been made so many times during the past few hours that they accepted it automatically, and smiled towards the stranger, expecting him to move to the next truck if given no encouragement to stay.

"Where are you from?" the stranger asked Morley.

"London," Morley said, without bothering to raise his head.

In turn the priest, in perfect English, asked each member of the section where he hailed from, and they felt obliged to answer. On receipt of their replies he enquired if their towns had remained unscathed after all the bombing, as he'd been informed by the Germans that they were all totally destroyed. When assured they were all standing, he seemed to be pleased.

"Ghent," he replied in answer to Morley's

question as to his own home town. He seemed to be a good and genuine man, and next day he was seen to spend a lot of time looking after the welfare of the wounded. It turned out he was a Jesuit, and studying in the order in Louvain. He pointed out that it took thirty two years of constant study before he could become a fully-fledged priest. During the course of conversation he hinted that he'd looked after several allied airmen when they'd been shot down, and kept them out of the clutches of the enemy.

They remained in Louvain for two days. On the way out of the town the column suddenly emerged onto a river bank. A shout from Morley drew their attention. "Look, there it is. That's the very position our forward platoon held in 1940. That's the very same bridge they had to cross to get back to us, under fire." He pointed to a rickety, single planked structure spanning the river. "That's the very spot where I was." He pointed to some buildings on the far side of the river. He continued to feed his eyes on the spot for as long as the speed of the column would allow. As he resumed his seat he kept muttering, "That's where company headquarters was...where he said "As long as there is a God on the throne, right would win"...four years after he was right. As the others by now were laughing at him, Morley with a sweep of his hand lapsed into moody silence, overcome with emotion.

Oatley for one realised what he was referring to, that night in the hut in Yorkshire, almost a year ago, when the dolls' house was under construction. The argument, and the prophecy...

As they drove on the signs of the enemy became virtually non-existent. Enquiries from locals at the roadside merely elicited a wave of the hand, and a new expression, 'Kaput, kaput.'

"Hmm, that's strange lingo, we must be in the Flemish speaking part of Belgium," said Copplestone.

This was endorsed by the signposts which were written not in French, but a strange language akin to German.

On they drove, unopposed till midday, when they entered some heavily-wooded country. Here a number of strongly held enemy positions slowed their advance. For several days the battalion assumed a defensive role, ready to abort any attempts of the enemy, who'd been cut off from their main units, from escaping. Little happened during that period, apart from the spectacle of a complete British Army Corps passing their position on their way to mop up the retreating enemy.

One evening the radio-operator on Spottiswoode's truck tuned into the B.B.C. news bulletin, where much to their delight they heard the announcer mention the part the division had played in the liberation of Brussels.

"We're actually in the news. Here's hoping our friends in Blighty heard it." shouted Spottiswoode.

Grayson was hoping that Holly Farm might have tuned in and be singing their praises.

For the next few days, because of some enemy opposition they advanced at a slower rate, then for a week they halted altogether. It was during this time that Grayson noticed a battered looking lorry approaching. When almost abreast, the driver tooted his horn. It turned out to be none other than his old mate Phelps. After the usual greeting Grayson enquired where Phelps had got the vehicle, for by the look of it, it wasn't the one issued to him. It seemed that Phelps' long-standing reputation for acquiring things without paying for them had once again asserted itself.

"Had it palmed off on me; just couldn't refuse." he grinned.

"Where's your old truck?"

"We hit a spot of bother the other night when we ran into a Jerry pocket of resistance, one of the ones you chaps left behind. Some of our wagons got hit, and mine was one of them." Phelps said.

Before he could expand further a shell dropped near by, so not wishing to lose this vehicle as well Phelps put his foot on the accelerator and moved off at a smart pace to take cover and to complete his mission of bringing supplies....

Chapter Fourteen

Meanwhile back in Yorkshire life had gone on for the Fentons, Hewletts and Aunt Elizabeth, indeed for all the village-folk, as normally as was possible under the circumstances. Since that unforgettable morning when the men they loved had driven away to fight, life for the most part had been humdrum. Hungry for any snippet of information covering the battalion's movements, they crowded around their radios each evening listening to news bulletins.

Eventually letters began to filter back, but these did not give a true picture of events, for any gruelling experiences referred to were worded in such a way as to betray neither the location nor the true feelings of the men. Though from the smears and marks on the paper it wasn't hard to conclude that they had been written at some battle-front.

Finally they were forced to develop the philosophy that 'no news is good news' as weeks went by with no mention of the battalion on the radio.

It was on one such evening that with dramatic suddeness, the name of the division was mentioned momentarily during a new bulletin. Though it was only the briefest mention, and in connection with the liberation of Brussels, it was sufficient to turn the village upside down. Doors were flung open and people rushed into the streets.

"Lorna, Lorna," shouted Clare Fenton, as she raced across the street to her friend who had appeared at her own door, "did you hear the news, the wonderful news?"

"Yes I did," said Lorna, tears welling up in her eyes.

"Isn't it wonderful, our dear lads?" Clare cried as she flung her arms around her friend's neck.

Soon they were lost in conversation about old times, and as they both talked at the same time the whole became delightfully incoherent.

"Oh, I do hope they're all right," Clare finished.

At that moment Mr Fenton appeared, flushed and panting. He said, "Someone said they'd make a name for themselves; you remember, the day they went off?"

'That's right," the girls said in unison.

"Well so they have; so they have." he panted holding onto Clare's arm in an attempt to get his breath back.

By this time other neighbours, including the Hewletts, had left their radio sets and had formed little groups in the street. All had the same topic of conversation. It was a real tonic to them – just what they needed.

"I wonder if Aunt Elizabeth's heard it?" Clare said.

"Let's go and find out," said Lorna.

Together they raced up the road, past the old seat, to the front door of Holly Farm.

"Heard the news?" they panted, as Aunt Elizabeth and her daughter appeared at the door.

Of course they'd heard it. There was little that Aunt Elizabeth didn't hear.

"The dear lads. God bless 'em." The old lady said, her voice heavy with emotion.

"He has already," Clare said.

"Aye, and He will some more, you'll see," the old lady replied.

Too excited to go in, the girls said good-night and sped off down the road together in the darkness.

It was a tired but happy village which eventually found its way to bed that night........

Chapter Fifteen

The dawn light had just begun to filter across the sky that Sunday morning as the company dragged itself out of fox-holes and from sandy fields and woods and quietly prepared for yet another attack. By now they were only a few miles south of the Dutch border, and they had been bivouacked for some days in the sand dunes, where they had been 'resting', if resting it could be called, for each day the artillery had kept up a constant barrage. But tried soldiers that they were, they had looked upon the few days respite as a breathing space before the next attack should swallow up their remaining energies.

Conscious of the significance of this Sunday morning, they were not above letting each other know their feelings.

"They say it's to be an easy one," said Vincent.

"They say so, but I've a feeling it won't be," Copplestone said cynically.

"We're going north through Holland anyway; reckon it's the easiest way to Germany," Morley said.

"Gather there's an army of paratroopers going in; that'll shake things up a bit. Glad I'm not one of them." Vincent said.

"We're still the leading division. I reckon we'll see some tough spots before we're through," Copplestone said comfortingly.

"What's the time?"

"Ten past ten."

"The Airborne crowd are due to drop in two hours' time," Morley said, doing a quick calculation.

"We'll be away any time after that. There's time to cook dinner before we move. Let's....."

"You, get your kit and prepare to move." an N.C.O. growled.

"Me, Sergeant?" stammered Morley.

"Yes, you. Get going. We've got to send half-a-dozen men to help reinforce two other companies; and you're one."

The N.C.O. moved off, leaving the men shaken.

"Just my foul luck, right through everything in this section and now I've got to leave you. It's too bad," Morley complained.

The others sympathised, but army life was too full of partings for there to be any point on dwelling on the situation. Shortly afterwards Morley marched off with the reinforcement detachment for the other companies. His mates wondered when they would see him again.

He arrived at B.H.Q. and was standing alone when amongst another reinforcement party he saw Percy Weatherall. It turned out that he had recovered from his injuries and had been detailed for the reinforcement camp ever since. They swapped notes, and beaming with pride Weatherall said, referring to the victorious drive to Brussels, "We heard at the camp you were advancing so quickly that you had got out of radio range, and we thought we'd find the war over before we caught up with you."

Morley laughed.

Soon the reinforcements were detailed onto waiting transport for their respective companies, Weatherall to his old company and Morley to a new one. They drove off to the sound of a heavy 'drum-fire' barrage, which had opened up to prepare the way for the advance. As Morley reached his new section an air-attack involving bombs and rockets livened up the proceedings, and soon afterwards the leading battle-group attacked.

Meanwhile Crabtree and Spottiswoode, through their vehicle radios, kept their immediate circle informed of events.

"The paratroopers have dropped," Crabtree said.

"Better eat quickly before we move," Vincent said.

"There's plenty of time, the battalion's not the first battle-group in the attack, we'll be some time yet," Crabtree said. He was right, for it was evening before they moved.

About two miles along the road they crossed a canal. What remained of daylight soon passed and night descended. They passed a convoy of vehicles loaded with bridging-kit. Despite the

116

care taken it was impossible to avoid, from time to time, scraping the sides of these trucks. Burning haystacks set on fire by Typhoons hurled a lurid yellow-red glare into the sky, providing welcome illumination for the drivers. On they pushed in fits and starts, and were now well inside Holland.

Presently a voice warned of mines ahead, and to keep to the centre of the road. Both columns jockeyed for position. Despite this warning the centre of the road could not be occupied by everyone at the same time so verges had to be risked. Soon these became squelching masses of mud. About midnight the bridging-parties harboured up, so this enabled the battalion once again to assume full ownership of the road. Only just in time, for several derelict armoured-cars betrayed the presence of the minefield. For once grateful for the rain which fell on the road surface to illuminate it like a silver streak, the anxious drivers kept off the verges and finally turned into a harbouring area, guided to it through the gloom by several burning haystacks.

Dead tired now, the companies set about the unpleasant task of digging slit-trenches against surprise attack. It was gruelling work, especially with empty bellies, tired backs and addled minds. Copplestone refused to dig, saying he would sleep in the truck. Vincent completed his trench, but then he too attempted to sleep in the truck. They had barely closed their eyes when a dull thud brought them both tumbling out of the truck and headlong into the trench. Within seconds, two faces under steel helmets was all that was visible of Vincent and Copplestone, above the parapet of the shallow fox-holes as they attempted to trace the noise.

"Jerry patrol with bazookas. They've sugared off now. Luckily they hit nothing," a voice came out of the darkness.

Copplestone and Vincent needed no second telling and within seconds had returned to the truck, where regardless of Jerry they spent the rest of the night. The pale grey light of morning, and the ominous boom of another victim falling

117

foul on the minefield, set them astir once more.

The column rolled onto the road and halted. Here they were told to wait till several objectives in front had been captured. This particular wait lasted for most of the day, but towards evening they were rewarded with a royal welcome from the inhabitants of a large town, recently liberated, who cheered wildly as the column sped through at dusk. Beyond the town they harboured for the night. The vehicles were in three lines as the section awaited its turn to harbour. An aeroplane was heard overhead, and many ducked as a dark shape loomed low over the crowded roadway. To the great relief of everyone it moved on without depositing any bombs.

"It must have been one of ours," Copplestone said.

"You don't say." Vincent said sarcastically.

Finally they were allowed to enter the harbouring area, where they halted and prepared for the night. They were told that engineers ahead were putting a bridge over a canal. It would be completed by the morning, and their company would be in the lead for the crossing.

Next morning they crossed the newly-built bridge, and headed northwards at full speed. The rising sun beamed its welcome, and paratroopers were everywhere, patrolling in jeeps or on foot. What opposition there was the paratroopers had already dealt with, and the column tore on.

"Jerry's bound to be festering in those," an N.C.O. said, pointing to a number of green areas on the map. "We'll have to fight through these woods, and that'll take some time."

"Bridge ahead." shouted Grayson as he peered through the vizor of his vehicle.

"There are three bridges altogether; the paratroopers have to capture the lot," the N.C.O. said, referring to his map.

The racing vehicles slowed as the huge structure came into view. A number of paratroopers ran out of a village adjacent to it and greeted them with howls of delight. Others from their fox-holes by the bridge, waved like excited children.

"Jerry's been shooting them up with mortars and they've only had rifles to hold them back; poor blighters, no wonder they're glad to see us." the N.C.O. said.

"They've done a terrific job taking this bridge and holding it," said Grayson, as he dribbled slowly over the bridge after Crabtree.

"Keep straight," the N.C.O. said, following the route on the map. "Hope the rest's as easy as that."

Five minutes driving brought them to the edge of a large town. The thunder of guns ahead and the premature halt filled them with trepidation regarding an unopposed entry.

"Anti-tank guns covering the road," observed Crabtree.

They were ordered to turn about and the whole column drove a short distance back towards the bridge, then took a detour to the left along a country road cluttered up with paratroopers, jeeps and equipment, while the fields on either side were packed with gliders, a number of which lay wrecked where they'd crash-landed. Like their comrades, these Airborne troops were delighted to see the column. Now they were equal to anything Jerry might throw at them. As the tanks ploughed past they whipped up clouds of dust which fell over the paratroopers. The column's speed increased, and for the next few miles they attained the highest speed of the advance so far. At one stage Grayson's speedometer registered over 40 m.p.h. Finally the mad sprint died down, and with a crash of gears and screams of braking tracks, the column swung onto a broad main road and halted.

A signpost said "Nijmegen 3 kilometres."

"Don't fancy this place much," Copplestone said.

The words were barely out of his mouth when a Typhoon attack in the distance filled the morning air with sounds of strife.

"Back up for Arnhem; it's over there," the N.C.O. said.

Soon a pitful trail of refugees came streaming out of Nijmegen, clinging to their belongings in a panic-stricken attempt to get away from the town before they became engulfed in the conflict.

Some of them remained close to the column, and the odd one who could speak English gave them the gruesome details of the past few days.

A forward fighting patrol was sent towards the town, and this included Hilton and Cragg. Uppermost in their minds was the information gleaned from one of the refugees that there were three thousand S.S. troops in the town. However it was not long before they returned, wearing confident smiles. Once they had been de-briefed the company turned onto another route, and after a short distance they halted outside a large monastery.

Some American Airborne troops were in evidence. In a field nearby, well camouflaged, was a battery of their 75mm. guns working overtime, pounding some enemy hidden in dense wooded countryside which predominated the area. The Americans gave them a great welcome and shared their chocolate ration. One of them, a linesman, updated Grayson on the situation and explained that their immediate objective was to capture the bridge over the Waal – and that so far all attempts had failed.

An uncomfortably long wait ensued while operational plans were being drawn up. This intermission afforded them an opportunity to 'mash-down', which was just as well, as no other occasion was to come their way in the immediate future. Finally the officers and N.C.O.'s were briefed, and the plan divulged to the men. It sounded hair-raising in the extreme, and consisted of the company plus tanks – less Hilton and Cragg's platoon – to make what was nothing less than a suicidal attempt to cross the mighty 600 yard wide bridge over the river Waal. The other platoon, with a back-up of tanks, was to rush the railway bridge lower down the river. Both plans contained all the ingredients for a 'death or glory' struggle.

The afternoon sun was already casting long shadows around them as they slipped down the road from the monastery. Realising the enormous issue at stake, not surprisingly everyone wore a grim expression.

"At least we've got two companies of American paratroopers with us for support," said a corporal on Oatley's truck, "makes you feel a bit better."

Undoubtedly it did improve the morale to see a line of paratroopers on either side of the road, jogging along on foot. Oatley glanced at the half-dozen tanks and bren-carriers keeping their distance in front of him.

'We're next for it after them,' he thought to himself. He looked around his mates, sitting silent, and almost bolt upright, their rifles and bren-guns tucked between their knees. The discipline they portrayed sent his spirits soaring sky-high.

"The bridge is thought to be mined; one of the other companies has been detailed to capture the building where the controls are," the N.C.O. briefed the section in his matter-of-fact way.

A shiver went down Oatley's spine. "What if they fail to capture it?" he asked curtly.

"Then it's just too bad for us." the man next him said.

"If we get across, then the rest of the division will follow - but if we don't, well, there's no order for that." the N.C.O. said.

The odds against a successful attempt to cross the bridge seemed overwhelming, but the column rattled on at a steady pace without opposition, and entered a residential part of the town, the streets of which were completely deserted. They skirted a small park, moved down several streets, then everything happened at once.

Whoomp. crunch...

A shower of heavy shells intended for a church, which was an Airborne observation post, skimmed the tops of some houses and exploded close enough to send clouds of smoke and dust over Oatley's vehicle. Almost simultaneously the leading tanks and bren-carriers opened up with their automatics, spraying each house in turn as they approached to liquidate snipers, who had begun to make their presence felt by single shots or bursts from small-arms, resulting in the smashing of all windows in the area. The column's marksmen managed to keep the snipers at bay until it turned the last corner before the bridge, when it became subjected to the most intense fire from every quarter. The third tank in line was the first victim, and it was obvious that Jerry had planned this so that it would successfully block the retreat of the others, which could then be dealt with at their leisure. The second tank was about to fire when the casing came off a round already in the breech, resulting in the tank becoming impotent, and making it a sitting target for the anti-tank guns which opened up. Though partially disabled, it managed to crawl around the corner, and take cover behind some buildings.

All this time the leading tank had been exposed to a merciless hail of anti-tank and bazooka fire, but its crew manfully fought back. Every time a heavy shell hit its hull a shower of sparks flew off it. This uneven fight could not be sustained indefinitely, and ultimately it fell victim. The bren-carriers, which had hovered in support of the tanks, realising that further action for the moment was impossible, joined the rest of the column behind the cover of some buildings.

To make matters worse, Oatley's platoon, which had pushed up close to support the tanks in their hour of need, now found themselves cut-off from their rear by anti-tank and machine-gun fire. The whole area became choked with smoke and flames from the burning tanks and buildings.

Through this chaos pushed a well-dressed man and woman, dragging between them a terrified elderly woman. The look of terror on all their faces was unforgettable, and they weren't long about seeking shelter down a side street.

Oatley's platoon was ordered to de-bus and take up position in some buildings overlooking the bridge, where they could fire with advantage on the enemy. Each man stood well back in the shadows and fired individually as best he could, until a shell hit the wall outside their building.

"We've been spotted." yelled Oatley.

Within seconds the platoon pulled out, and moved into fresh cover before the next shell found its mark. Meanwhile the other platoon had held firm in their vehicles until ordered to take cover. Unable to advance any further without running the gauntlet of the enemy's fire, they waited for the next move. A silence fell over the position, broken only by the clang of a stretcher-bearer truck.

"A hundred to one it gets hit," someone said, as they watched it roar over the crossroads. Its sides became peppered with machine-gun fire, but no anti-tank gun opened fire. Finally it gained the cover of the building.

Just then a section of American paratroopers approached and headed for the bridge. Fearful that they would be caught in the vicious enemy fire, the British hurled several smoke grenades into the centre of the road; this gave the paratroopers just enough cover to enable them to double across the road, with machine-gun bullets whizzing about their heels. One man's helmet fell off and he ran back to recover it, despite the fusillade which greeted this act.

By now the crossroads was nearly as hot a spot as the corner nearest the bridge. Oatley watched another armoured-car gathering speed to attempt a crossing. It was Spottiswoode's. Oatley held his breath as he watched it hugging the shelter of the houses, until with a few yards to go it accelerated and shot across the road, with a stream of bullets pouring from its bren-gun. To the accompaniment of wild cheering from the British, it made it to safety.

With the coming of darkness they consolidated their position. The enemy made no attempt to counter-attack, but kept up a constant barrage from their heavy guns. The town of Nijmegan was shrouded in darkness apart from the glare from the river bank which marked the spots where the two bridges were being attacked. Eventually the very long night ended, and with the coming of dawn came the order to move back into the trucks.

After some minutes' drive they re-formed near a small park.

123

"What's this all about?" asked someone.

"We're going to attack, of course," snapped Oatley as his temper began to fray due to the severe tension built up during the night.

Enemy guns ranged in, and several men became casualties.

"The town must be cleared, then we can attack the bridge; that is if Jerry hasn't blown it up by then," Crabtree said.

"We're going in on foot, with only three vehicles; any more would present too big a target," a sergeant said.

Morley's new company led the attack, but Oatley and his crew had only ten minutes to wait before it was their turn. By way of cover their own guns and mortars were raining down a sea of shells on the enemy position. They dashed across a main road, crept towards a market-place, hugging the houses. Quickly deploying, each platoon set about clearing the houses as it went. Any enemy occupying these quickly retreated, and a vicious sniping match took its toll of the attackers. Neither side sought quarter, and when shooting took place it was always savage.

Yard by yard the company advanced and never eased up till the street which was their objective was reached. Here they took cover in basements, or behind walls, while Jerry raked every inch of ground with machine-gun fire.

"This is real hell on earth," gasped a man behind Catley.

"I haven't been so scared since the 'Spud Patch', but we've got them taped," Oatley said.

"They're still fighting like mountain cats," someone else said.

For a time all went quiet; then another burst of vicious fire from the enemy. Stillness and chaos alternated all morning, and it was the stillness which generated the most fear.

All this was bound to claim victims. In one instance while one platoon was holding the ground it had won, sniper shots continued to come from the interior of a shop on the far side of the road. With a disregard for his own safety amounting to recklessness, Calder moved towards the spot. A shot rang out and hit him. Bellowing with pain he rushed forward and emptied his automatic through the shop window.

"I got him. He got me first, but I got him." he kept repeating, and beckoned to his section to come forward to help him. By the time they reached him he was in considerable pain – he'd been shot clean through the leg. But he'd done his duty and got his section out of a tight spot.

A further deluge of shells hit the ground as Calder and several other wounded were being loaded onto a bren-carrier. Calder lay in the back of the vehicle in a state of unnatural bliss – hadn't he both done his duty and received a wound, which, though painful, was not serious; the direct consequence of which would get him out of the front line and into a field hospital.

Grayson had hardly recovered from watching the exuberant Calder depart when Vincent arrived grinning all over his face.

"I've just had peaches and cream," he laughed.

"Peaches and cream? Where did you get those in this hellhole?"

"You remember that last lot of shelling?"

Grayson nodded.

"Well I dived into a cellar for shelter, and bumped into a Dutch family, who thought I was coming to shoot them. When they discovered I wasn't they were so relieved that they opened up some jars of peaches and cream, and shared them."

"What a war; on one hand blokes are being killed right, left and centre, and here you are stuffing yourself with peaches and cream." Grayson slapped his friend on the shoulder.

Just then Weatherall's company came up to help clear the town. With the minimum of greeting they moved off on their task and soon disappeared among the maze of buildings, which quickly rang with the sound of their automatics. They shot up everything in sight, and challenged Jerry to come out to fight. On they pushed with showers of shrapnel splattering around them. Finally a halt was called in preparation for the final phase of the attack on the great bridge itself. Grayson and Vincent spoke momentarily to Morley, who passed in his armoured car. He was able to tell them that the bridge was still intact, and that Phelps and Henshaw were running a bus service with ammunition from B.H.Q. to the mortars covering the bridge.

Relieved, Grayson and Vincent were ordered to stand fast with their section, but Oatley was not so fortunate, for without warning he found himself tearing along with the rest to the end of the street from which they would emerge for the assault. They reached it just as the attack was beginning. Smoke from burning buildings and exploding grenades partially obscured his view, but as he crouched behind a wall Oatley could make out what looked like a large ancient fort. As the smoke cleared he could see enemy fire coming from the apertures in the side.

"We must capture this place before we tackle the bridge," a sergeant said grimly. "The other companies are closing in - get that bren-gun cracking." He pointed to a group of enemy at the front of the fort.

Oatley ranged on them, and this was followed up by a barrage of British shells, which forced Jerry to keep his head down. Seizing their opportunity, the attackers crept forward or doubled from cover to cover in short dashes. A tank fired a lucky shot at one of the apertures, penetrating inside and doing tremendous damage. Despite suffering a considerable number of casualties, Morley's new company pressed forward and gained the enemy positions outside the fort.

Oatley's section continued to advance and give covering fire. The fort itself still remained to be taken, but by this time Weatherall's company was advancing rapidly from another flank. Through a hail of bullets they pushed and eventually gained the entrance to the fort. By now every weapon possible was ranged and fired at the entrance, and under cover of this Weatherall and half-a-dozen other worthies with fixed bayonets rushed in.

In no time the enemy defenders were defeated, and this was attributable in no small measure to

126

the performance of a PIAT gunner, who sent bomb after bomb hurtling into the dark interior of the fort. Palls of smoke hung around everything, and darkness had fallen; however there remained sufficient light for Oatley to notice five tanks streak out from under cover of some buildings.

"Here, where are they off to?" he shouted.

"Crikey, they're charging up the ramp of the bridge - a suicide bid if ever I saw one." someone shouted.

"There they go, they're firing their Beza's.."

Tracer-bullets licked the framework of the great bridge. Thud...a dull note resounded through the bridge.

"They've blown the bridge...they're..."

"It's not the bridge, it's our tanks, they've been hit," the sergeant roared.

Another thud was audible, followed by a flash – then silence...

Presently a message over the radio clarified the position. It transpired that German guns had knocked out three of the British tanks, but the others had got across. Allied paratroopers had also crossed the river in boats lower down and were in the process of linking up with the tanks.

"The bridge is won." yelled Oatley.

"All ours. The impossible has happened," the sergeant said.

Within minutes the battle-scarred town was full of troops - men and vehicles were everywhere. Other units had joined them and pushed their way into Nijmegan. The change from enemy occupied to Allied control seemed the most natural thing in the world. Apart from several uncontrolled fires in buildings the battle, like some violent hurricane, had blown itself out. All that was left was the background noise of the guns at Arnhem, where a fierce fight still raged.

When Nijmegen awoke next morning it was to sunshine. Unable to remain hidden in cellars any longer the people flooded into the street. Shops opened and business premises were unlocked. As usual the troops became the recipients of gifts and praise. At noon orders came through for a move back out of the town – for a rest period.

But as usual the rest period was curtailed by the arrival of Crabtree's truck the next day.

"We're packing up, we're moving. They say it's a small clearing up operation, but I don't like the sound of it," he said sullenly.

The official order soon followed and off they moved in formation, back over the same route they'd come.

"What's going on now?" moaned Vincent.

"Jerry's at the road behind us, we've to clear it up," the N.C.O. said.

It was a very disconsolate Vincent who stood in a trench that night with the rain soaking him through, staring into space. For all he knew or cared Jerry could be on all sides of him. However, by way of compensation, next day the road-clearing operation went through with the minimum of resistance. Despite this no one was under any illusion that they'd seen the last of Jerry as the surrounding woods were reputed to be full of him. From time to time bursts of sporadic fire issued from these woods, but as they grew less and less it became obvious that the enemy was in retreat.

Unfortunately Cragg, who was just returning from a patrol, got hit by a sniper's bullet which went straight through his thigh and out the other side. He was in considerable pain as they lifted him onto the stretcher, after binding his legs together with two enormous shell dressings clamped over the wound. Conscious, he attempted to wave good-bye to his mates as the stretcher-bearer jeep moved off, for it would be a long time before they saw him again.

For his mates left behind, another week of tough fighting had to be endured before they got rest. "If it's like this here, what must it have been like at Arnhem?" Vincent said.

Chapter Sixteen

"This would remind you of the old hut in Yorkshire, wouldn't it?" Rattray said.

"Doesn't half; just think, barely a year ago we were 'on production' there. Time sure flies when you're enjoying yourself." Grayson laughed.

"What about starting another dolls' house now, Phelps?"

Phelps shook his head several times and puffed thoughtfully at his pipe. His whole expression indicated that he'd lost all enthusiasm for that particular idea.

"Well, with all you blokes here, it does remind me of the old hut," Rattray persisted. Silence. Refusing to be subdued, he persevered, "In fact it is the first official reunion we've had since the Yorkshire days, this hut's a home from home."

"Home. When will we see it again?" said Phelps, breaking his silence. "A shocking lot has happened since we were all together in Blighty." He dropped his voice. "There's a few old faces missing for a start."

"Which reminds me, I've had a letter from Cragg," Hilton said.

"How's he doing?"

"Still in plaster, and will always walk with a limp, but otherwise O.K."

"Well, suffering binds us all together, and heaven knows we've all suffered enough since we left England, even if we haven't been wounded," Phelps said.

"How long have we been here?" Cunningham asked.

"It's six weeks since we came out of action. Then we spent three weeks camping in the woods, two in billets on the main road, and now here," Hilton said, looking thoughtful.

"In other words we're due for a move; we'll not be left here in peace much longer." said Rattray.

He scanned the room uneasily; the thought of having to vacate it when the time came was not pleasing. It was not much of a place when all was said and done, but it was a lot better than many soldiers were enjoying. It was a backroom of a farmhouse in Southern Holland. The front line was only a few miles away, and gun-fire was constantly audible.

"Wonder where we'll go next? I reckon we'll have another crack at Arnhem," Rattray said.

"What makes you say that?" Cunningham said curtly.

"Oh I don't know, I've just got a feeling. For instance last night when I was on sentry, I watched a stack of German rockets somewhere up north, headed out to sea, ir the direction of British cities. We must stop them. That's why I think we'll go north again.

They prepared to 'mash down'. Cunningham opened a surviving tin of German bread.

"No thanks, one lot of that stuff's quite enough for me," Hilton said.

Phelps eyes twinkled." I'll tell you the story of that bread. When the road was cut that time and supplies were stopped, someone found a Jerry supply depot. The Service Corps commandeered it. But the funny thing is, unbeknown to them our people drew rations from it, and each morning when they'd left Jerry turned up and drew his rations; neither side knew till it was all over."

"That beats Vincent's peaches and cream into a cocked hat." Hilton shook with laughter.

Finally the party broke up, and Hilton and Grayson returned to their quarters nearby. They had barely settled in before the information filtered through that they were to move the next night at 1900 hours. The remarkable accumulation of kit and extras from a six weeks rest period required considerable effort to dispose of, but they managed it on time and the next evening found them moving, not north as Rattray had predicted, but in a southerly direction. They steeled themselves for the inevitable night drive, and altogether the move took a day and a night, and culminated in a small township.

Spottiswoode, who'd been sent with the advance party, greeted them on arrival. "We're here for one night only, then it's onto the line," he said curtly.

"An attack?"

"No we're to hold a forward position; it appears we're facing part of the defences of the Siegfried Line."

Grayson went to sleep that night wondering what surprises the much talked of 'Siegfried Line' held for them. It was a small comfort that they were involved in operations on only an extension of the line, the main defences being further south.

Next day the company was briefed. The orders were many and varied. In essence the company was to move forward in the afternoon, halt at another small town till dusk, then they were to advance on foot to the forward position. Any optimism which had grown on the part of the drivers was soon dashed when six vehicles were ordered to move to the forward line by 0200 hours, by which time the infantry would be under cover in the trenches. The drivers included Crabtree, Hilton, Grayson and Spottiswoode.

Finally they were ready. Still in Holland, they crossed the German border where they halted till dusk. Then, heavily laden with kit, the platoons set off on foot for their night march across country. Within the hour they'd reached their destination and relieved the unit currently occupying the sector. They settled down in a wintry atmosphere, eyes and ears strained for the slightest movement from 'No Man's Land', which was the only thing separating them from Jerry. So far all had gone according to plan. All that was required now was the arrival of the six vehicles. This the men in the trenches dreaded, for the noise of their engines would be a signal for enemy shelling.

Meanwhile the drivers, who had been joined by another truck, waited nervously in the rear. Several times during this unpleasant waiting period they heard shells dropping along the route they had to take.

Finally at zero hour they formed up, Crabtree leading, followed by Hilton and Grayson, with Spottiswoode bringing up the rear. Most of the vehicles were towing anti-tank guns or trailers, which further reduced their manoeuvrability.

"Keep close up and be ready to turn right when we reach the church in the next village," the N.C.O. said.

Crabtree moved off at a high speed, almost as if he'd forgotten that others were attempting to follow. Roads and fields looked alike in the night fog, with the result that the column narrowly missed ditches on three or four occasions and those in the rear had the greatest difficulty in keeping up with the main body. Grayson was beginning to wonder how long he could hold out when he saw Hilton halt suddenly. This caused him to brake violently.

"I've lost the column." Hilton said desperately.

"I'm not surprised, that idiot Crabtree's going far too fast — he's driving like a maniac," Grayson said.

"We must be due to turn right about here, at the church?"

"That looks like it ahead." Hilton moved forward on foot to investigate.

"Looks like a church ahead," he called softly, as he jumped back into his truck.

They moved forward into a village, in the centre of which they could just see the dim shape of a church. A road branched off to the right. Hilton followed it for a few yards, then halted.

"There's no sign of 'em." he called to Grayson.

The rear party closed up and Spottiswoode joined them in the road.

"Where are we going to?" rasped Hilton, frustrated almost beyond endurance.

"This is the road we were ordered to turn up, that's all I know," said Spottiswoode, gazing at the derelict village.

"Supposing it isn't, we'll end up in Jerry lines." fumed Hilton.

Two figures emerged from a building.

"Get your trucks off that corner and be sharp about it." one called out, before the drivers had a chance to determine whether they were friend or foe.

"Who are you?" called out Grayson.

"Sentries. Our company took over here last

night, and the corner you are parked on was shelled only an hour ago."

"Have you seen three trucks?" enquired Grayson.

"No. We've been at the other end of the village."

At that moment they heard an engine ticking over.

"Listen."

Hilton and Grayson crept cautiously up the road to investigate. "There they are," whispered Grayson, pointing to a dark object ahead. "Get the others quick."

Another minute and they had joined up with Crabtree. It appeared he had been stopped by some sentries, and it was only then that he discovered they were missing, so he marked time till they caught up.

The final mile of the journey still remained. By now it was 0230 hours. Crabtree led, slower this time. It was almost blind driving, with only an occasional telegraph pole to mark the route.

Every yard brought them nearer their waiting colleagues and the listening enemy. Everything seemed very quiet. Crabtree knew that the noise of his engine must be reverberating from the bare fields like a hundred drums. The tension became unbearable. Suddenly he thought he could see houses. On he roared, with the pack on his tail. The road turned, a pond glistened in the gloom. The shapes of battered houses, still standing, became clearer. They roared into the deserted hamlet and halted. Orders were issued in an undertone. The anti-tank guns were unhitched and swiftly manhandled into position.

Surely the enemy must react soon.

Crabtree was ordered to drive his vehicle to a covered position. The others followed. One truck stalled and had to be towed. A Very light flickered up across a field. The enemy must be going to retaliate at last. The shattering exhaust noise of their vehicles died away as they reached their positions. Not a sound was heard......

Next day they discovered the lack of enemy retaliation.

"Even our own people didn't hear us come in,"

said Crabtree.

"They must have," Spottiswoode said, "Their trenches are so close."

"Not a sound, the wind must have been blowing in the wrong direction – it's a miracle, our prayers were answered after all." Crabtree said, as he looked towards the sky in awe.

"No doubt about that. If they'd attacked they'd have had us all for sure," Spottiswoode said, nodding his head.

For the next seven nights they shivered in the trenches. Their sector remained quiet but they were able to witness the awesome spectacle of a British bombardment, with hundreds of guns working overtime and the sky turning a lurid red as an advance went on to their right flank. A respite of several days back in reserve followed, then another turn in the line. This time the drivers were swapped, and Hilton and Grayson got a taste of what a night march could do to their feet. They soon acquired the art of treading noiselessly on grass verges, and other old foot soldiers' tricks. They got a rude shock when an odd shape behind them gave them an attack of the jitters. It turned out to be a cow which one of the men had commandeered, and in turn it supplied fresh milk. So successful was this operation that they took the beast with them when they left the position.

A third and final line operation came along before the company was withdrawn to a rest area.

"Well, at least we survived the Siegfried guns after all," Vincent said after it was all over.

"True." someone replied.

But not much else was said, for the truth of the matter was that all the tension and suffering in the cold at listening posts, in trenches, or on night patrols, were far too sensitive a subject even to be joked about, at least for the present.

Chapter Seventeen

"Hi you blokes, haven't seen you for ages."

"Well, if it isn't old Percy. How's it going?"

"Could be worse, a bit browned off perhaps, "said Weatherall, a huge grin splitting his face.

"What have you got to be browned off about?" said Henshaw disapprovingly.

"Well, for a start I hear that leave back to Blighty starts next month, but I'm at the bottom of the list."

"I'm like you, they drew the names out of a hat," said Grayson.

"I gather there's an inter-company drill competition this week; that should be fun," Weatherall said, changing the subject.

This and other mundane subjects constituted a pre-church parade conversation on a foggy December morning. The drill competition was upon them before they knew it, and every afternoon of the following week was given up to drill parades.

"Well there's one consolation, I hear we're going back to Brussels for Christmas, to re-fit," said Spottiswoode.

"A likely story," said Crabtree.

One evening they were discussing this rumour and others, when someone switched the radio on. It was turned to Hamburg, and soon the smooth tones of Lord Haw-Haw filled the room.

..."Our troops have broken through the enemy's line, and are advancing at lightning speed..." the voice droned on.

"What does he take us for?" yelled Crabtree, "he must...."

The door opened, and an officer appeared.

"Prepare to move in half-an-hour. The enemy has broken through the American front and an attack is anticipated on this front too," he said quietly.

As he spoke there was an increase in the noise of gunfire, and the windows rattled ominously.

The officer withdrew, leaving behind a hutful of speechless and bewildered men.

"Half-an-hour?" gasped Grayson eventually.

"Someone shut that creep off, he's right for

once." an N.C.O. said. Crabtree switched the radio off.

Immediately there was a vast amount of activity in the hut, as the packing of kit became a priority.

"That's the end of the Brussels leave yarn," Crabtree said.

"And the drill competition," added Spottiswoode happily.

Despite the order to stand-by, they did not move all that night, nor all the next day. An inordinate number of jokes were made to the effect that they were actually standing-by to go on leave to Brussels after all. It was not till evening that they learnt their fate. After briefing the officers and platoon sergeants, the men were quietly informed of what was required of them.

The briefing N.C.O. said, "You've heard, no doubt, of the enemy push against the Yanks. We've got to go down and get involved. We don't know exactly what is happening, but we must drive all night till we reach our destination. That's all; get on your vehicles and prepare to move out immediately, our company's to lead."

"Wow, so that's it." whistled Spottiswoode.

Whatever the terrors of the night would reveal, the traditional order of march was unbroken; Spottiswoode, Crabtree, Grayson. Slowly they moved off. Morley gave the 'thumbs-up' sign as they passed his company; so did Weatherall as his prepared to follow.

The thick shroud of fog which enveloped the whole of Southern Holland that December evening became denser as they moved along the road and crossed a pontoon bridge spanning the river Maas, which was already badly swollen with the extra rain of the past few weeks. Once across their speed increased, and this did nothing to help their freezing bodies and feet. For an hour they drove in silence through the night.

"Things don't look too good," Copplestone said at last.

"No, there's too many vehicles from other divisions, all headed in the same direction for my liking," the N.C.O. said.

136

Suddenly Grayson started. "Say, Crabtree must be having a night off, or be drunk; his tail-light's swinging from one side of the road to the other."

Grayson was in the relief driver's seat, and with the thick fog reducing visibility to zero he had stood up with his head and shoulders out of the top of the vehicle, in an attempt to direct his deputy. On each vehicle behind a man was similarly posted, but despite this the strain on the drivers was very severe, yet they performed their task admirably. Just then the fog began to lift, and to Grayson's relief this coincided with the straightening up of Crabtree's vehicle.

"Keep your eyes skinned for gun-flashes, then you'll know we're not far from the action," Vincent advised.

Two hours passed. They approached a town, drew into the main street and halted. It was already packed with enquiring civilians, all chattering in Flemish. Lights flashed from doors and windows, so that the whole scene resembled a reception rather than a chance visit brought about by the exigencies of war.

"No, we're not retreating," Copplestone assured a worried looking civilian.

"They can't make out why we're coming through in such force," Vincent said.

Within minutes they were on the move again. Across their route in front a vicious red light flickered as it travelled from east to west. It was followed by several others.

"V.I.s" yelled Grayson.

"Must be all part of the enemy push," Vincent said.

The next town was in complete darkness as they rattled through its empty streets. The night was now beautifully clear and the next few miles were easy going. A procession of flying-bombs began to pass almost directly overhead, and from all around the crackle of ack-ack guns was continuous. Nothing else was heard, and no other indications of battle were obvious. It was all very puzzling, even more so when they again halted with the object of harbouring for the night.

"We're in the hotel for the night," chuckled Crabtree, after the vehicles had been driven into an orchard.

He led the way to a barge barn, where it wasn't long before several platoons were making themselves comfortable in the hay, despite the abundant evidence of rats.

When they awoke the fog was collecting again.

"Get out onto the road," came the swift order. "Intelligence reports indicate Jerry has not crossed the river during the night. Our recce units are holding the bridges there, and we're now moving several miles to take up a defensive position," an N.C.O. briefed them quickly.

An American army truck drove past them. At the sight of the British column its half-dozen occupants burst out into shattering laughter.

"What about your London taxi-cabs now?" one of them shouted.

The British drivers were not prepared for this American wisecracking, nor the unruffled manner they were displaying with Jerry so close. By the time they'd recovered their composure and before they had an answer ready the truck was out of sight.

The short journey was covered without incident, and they took up defensive positions and consolidated. Accommodation proved to be a bit of a problem till Grayson and Copplestone found a comfortable cafe, but were soon moved to a much less comfortable billet beside the others.

It was here that they received the unpleasant attentions of a priest, who, after introducing himself in perfect English, said, "Are you running away?"

"Running away? We don't run away," snapped Vincent.

"Then what have you come down here for? The enemy has broken through. You'd better do something," the priest said with a smile.

Vincent replied that they were doing something, and boiling with rage at the priest's attitude, stormed off to tell Copplestone.

After inspecting the array of tanks and other vehicles with more than natural curiosity, the priest entered the house, and drawing up a chair, watched every movement of the section as it settled in.

"Don't like the look of him," said Copplestone, after he'd inspected the priest. "In 1940 Jerry dropped paratroopers into Holland dressed as priests. He could be one, especially as we've heard they have been dropping paratroopers behind the American lines. Keep you mouths shut, tell him nothing."

After a while the priest left the house, and the section lost no time in making friends with the inmates of their billet. Flying bombs continued to range overhead, and the occasional one dropped in the vicinity. Rumours of the enemy's progress continued to flow in. After three days of this static war, Spottiswoode said "I can't make this out; Jerry can't be making much headway."

"The Yanks must be fighting like mad," Grayson said.

"The RAF haven't been exactly idle either, there's been hundreds of planes overhead each day," Vincent said.

The priest continued to put in regular appearances. More than once he criticised the manner in which the Allies were fighting the Germans.

"Can't make the bloke out at all. Now it's every evening he comes, and stays at least two hours." Vincent said.

"Perhaps he's scared we'll pervert his flock." Grayson giggled.

"Where's he from?"

"Near Louvain."

"What? Never."

"Let him roast," roared Copplestone suddenly in a fit of impatience. "Don't you blokes realise it's Christmas Eve? Why worry about him."

"Aye, and we're going to have Christmas Dinner to-morrow, they're decorating the hall up the road to-night in preparation. Of course anything can happen between now and to-morrow to alter that," Grayson said.

But nothing did, and the celebration took place

at the appointed time. Everyone brought along his weapon in case of emergencies, but apart from that a good celebration was had by all.

Two days later word got around that short leave in Brussels was to be allowed after all, on the basis of two men per platoon at a time. Each man was to present his leave claim. A roll was drawn up and in the course of the next few days most of the mates got a turn.

Meanwhile an incident took place which concerned the priest. He still came and went, but on each visit the atmosphere grew more hostile and a clash became inevitable.

"I hear the Americans have held the Germans," he remarked casually one day.

Several men nodded.

"It's just as well. I'm glad 1940 was not repeated."

"That would never have happened," someone said.

"It might have, then what would we have done?"

"We would have fought to the last, that's what." Vincent said.

"What could a few men and tanks have done?" the priest sneered.

"There's a lot more besides what you see here," someone said.

"Well you might have left us, as you did in 1940."

"That was only after a fight."

"Not much of a fight," the priest said.

"What about those people who gave their lives then?" Grayson's temper was roused.

The argument hotted up and tempers became on edge. The whole section was drawn together in the room.

"Don't laugh at 1940." Copplestone shouted, "I was in it. I fought there. I was one of the lucky ones. I came through. Don't forget we were still fighting long after you'd surrendered."

"Belgium should have surrendered before she did," the priest flung back.

Considering that Belgium surrendered in the very early days of the campaign, this remark was altogether too much for the Spud Patch veterans, and victors of Nijmegen.

"Leave politics out of this and stick to your job, religion," shouted one soldier angrily.

"I'm more educated than you are, don't forget," the priest said.

The argument waxed hotter and more personal.

"Education is no guarantee of religion. Conduct alone indicates what a man is," Grayson fumed.

Realising that he was cornered, the priest retaliated, "You need to study more. If you think you're religious, study.....study the Bible."

By now the argument had been reduced to a feud between Grayson and the priest, with the former's mates backing him from a distance.

Finally, realising he was getting the worst of it, the priest stood up to go. Sullenly he backed towards the door, still declaring that Grayson was ignorant.

A member of the section opened the door and helped him on his way with a well aimed push.

Later, Vincent said, "I still can't make out his identity. What a difference between him and the other priest of Louvain."

The unfeeling attitude of the priest created more than sufficient fuel for the discussion to continue well on into the night.

Leave parties came and went. until one day a reshuffle of billets gave cause for speculation on future operations. It turned out that the companies were to take it in turns to visit a selected area some miles away, for field exercises.

"Phew, in this weather too," groaned Copplestone, viewing the countryside with its thick blanket of snow.

"So the Jerry offensive is over then?" Crabtree queried an N.C.O.

"More or less. The Yanks gave them all they needed. Their Airborne troops, who fought with us at Nijmegan, saved the day."

A week of intensive training followed, at the end of which they were very tired. But it was preferable to being in the front line.

The re-shuffle of billets had benefited some, for now Henshaw and Cunningham with Phelps and

Rattray had come within walking distance of the other companies. This resulted in things being a bit more homely than they'd been for sometime.

But one particularly cold and dreary morning, when spirits were at a low ebb, the rumour spread like wildfire that someone from the group had been killed. On further investigation, to the total horror of the friends it turned out to be Weatherall.

"Weatherall?" Henshaw gasped, when Cunningham told him. "Surely not. Whatever happened?"

"It's true. Killed outright on an exercise. Run over by a bren-carrier."

Grayson was completely overcome with grief when he heard.

"The last time I saw Percy was that morning on church-parade, when he was browned-off about his leave. Now he'll never go on leave, poor old Percy. Just imagine, he came through all that action, only to be killed on exercise."

"A brave man," was Hilton's tribute, "one I shall never forget."

Chapter Eighteen

The same day that the battalion took up its defensive position on the road to the Maas, another unit drew into a village several miles to the rear. Immediately its members began to unload their kit and take possession of such accommodation as there was. Within two hours the unit had settled in to what was to become an excellent winter quarter. They stood by to await reports and developments from the front line.

Inside one of these billets a white faced soldier stamped his chilly feet. His drawn expression and sunken eyes denoted fatigue sustained from a prolonged night drive. If his external appearance was not up to much, his internal condition was very much worse. Presently he was seized with an attack of shivering, followed by a fever, in which his face and hands broke out in a cold sweat. A second attack a few minutes later convinced Thorpe - for that's who it was - that he must report sick. There and then he reported to the M.O. and did not set foot in his newly acquired billet again for two weeks, but instead found himself inside a military hospital.

It was four days before Christmas, and not unnaturally his thoughts turned homewards. He attempted to get a mental picture of every Christmas he'd ever had since he was a small boy, up to last year, when for a brief spell he'd been so happy with Hilary. He thought of his mates, so near and yet so far, and wondered when he would see them again.

On Christmas Day, with the ward gaily decorated, he was feeling a little homesick when something fluttered down onto his pillow. It was an envelope. The mail was being handed out, and he recognised the post mark immediately.

Eagerly he tore it open; it was a Christmas card depicting a family around the Yule log, with snow piled high outside their house. The heat which the cheerful fire appeared to be throwing out transmitted itself to Thorpe and set his face aglow. He turned the page and read the greeting;

underneath was written 'From the Hewlett Family'.

So he was not alone after all. He was still very much alive in their hearts...

After Christmas he convalesced for a few days, then returned to his unit. A week later the Christmas card was followed by a letter from the Hewletts, describing their Christmas celebrations and mentioning how keenly they'd missed him. On his return he was resticted to light duties which consisted for the most part of driving. One morning he was in the act of turning off the main road towards his quarters when he noticed some trucks parked on the roadside.

"Hey." bawled a voice.

He slowed.

"Where are you stationed?"

He looked around and recognised Cunningham. He dared not stop, but pointed in the direction of his billet, hoping that Cunningham would tell his mates, so they could arrange a reunion.

A week passed, and when there was no sign of any of them he became despondent, and began to lose interest in his duties.

One evening he'd just been detailed for guard, and was sorting out his kit when the door opened and a strange figure, dressed in denim with a leather jerkin over the top entered. For a moment Thorpe didn't know him, but all of a sudden recognition dawned.

"Don." he shouted.

"Found you at last," Grayson replied.

They shook hands, and delighted in each other's company.

"I never thought we'd meet again till the war was over," Thorpe said.

"The funny thing is, we've been close to each other all the time, but not close enough to make contact. Will you ever forget that day in Bayeux, the steak and chips...?" Grayson laughed.

"We've all travelled a long way since then."

Grayson updated him on the welfare of his mates, but when he came to mention Weatherall he was unable to look Thorpe straight in the face.

"Grand chap Percy," Thorpe finally said, when he managed to speak. "Do you remember that day in York with Ruth and Hilary?"

Seizing the opportunity to change the subject, Grayson enquired about the girls.

"I've had letters from all of them," Thorpe drew himself up proudly. "Their card sure cheered me up on Christmas Day, when I was in 'Dock'."

"A fine time you chose."

"It suited well enough at the time, what with the icy weather and all.."

A clinking of brasses from the next room reminded Thorpe that he was supposed to be on guard.

"A fine time for you to call old lad, when I've got to go." he said.

"Never mind, I know where you are now. I'll come back with some of the lads," Grayson said as he took his leave.

Thorpe went to his post feeling lighter in spirit than he had done for a very long time.

Chapter Nineteen

"Where the thunder are we now; what's the name of this place?" someone shouted.

The clattering of engines and the screech of tracks died away in the streets of the town. The last units of the division arrived as dusk fell on them. As each vehicle halted, grimy, worn out men tumbled out onto flagged pavements, calling out for their billets. All and sundry were completely fagged out by the drive, which had taken up an entire day and was accomplished in thick fog and penetrating cold. Great secrecy had prevailed throughout, for they were moving from that area of Belgium to which the German winter counter-offensive had brought them. A mere handful knew where they were headed, but now, as they came to a dead stop in the large town, even the least intelligent knew instinctively that they had arrived at their destination.

"Tilburg." shouted a jeep-driver, in answer to the question. "Tilburg -- Holland."

"Tilburg," repeated Vincent. "What's to do here, action?"

The driver nodded, "We're here till Friday at least."

"That's great, we'll have a few days to sort ourselves out," Copplestone said.

Together with Vincent they proceeded to a house which had been pointed out to them as their quarters. By the time the remainder of the section had joined them they were comfortably billeted with a Dutch family, and had already downed several cups of tea which the good lady had made from their own rations.

A stout, middle-aged man sat in one corner of the room, quietly observing the new-comers who had settled down in his home with such alacrity. By his expression he regarded the whole business with considerable distaste. Several young girls attempted to engage the Tommies in conversation. This proved difficult, as neither side had mastered enough of the other's language to make it a viable proposition. Everything was 'gut' or 'nix-gut', while 'kaput' was thrown in for good measure and did fit into an incredible number of instances, and provided a yardstick for description for countless things.

Soon the atmosphere in the room mellowed, and even the austere head of the house began to unfreeze, especially when the men opened more of their rations and shared them around, for their hosts' cupboards had been painfully bare for more months than they cared to remember.

That night hundreds of families in Tilburg were similiarly hosting British soldiers. Indeed it soon became quite the thing, and was considered a dishonour not to have at least several soldiers billeted on them.

Friday came and went with not the slightest sign of a fresh move. Crabtree, acting as a self-appointed information officer, was able to assure his mates that they would remain in Tilburg for some time yet.

"A big attack has started, it's between the Rhine and the Maas; they reckon the battlefield's a quagmire, so we've orders to wait."

Nobody minded waiting, with Tilburg catering more than adequately for their welfare. They were out of sound of gunfire, and the only destructive elements were the VI's. These were quite frequent, and zoomed over the town in a southerly direction.

All in all there was plenty of work to do, but usually the evenings were free. It was during one of these evenings that Henshaw mentioned to Grayson that Thorpe had been seen in the town. "He's somewhere in that direction," Henshaw pointed towards the far side of Tilburg. "I'd say if you go to the next corner, turn left, walk half a mile, turn left again, you'll be in the vicinity of his unit."

"O.K. I'll look him up. You know I'd actually found him in Belgium and intended to see him again, but we moved before I got a chance. Twice this happened, in Bayeux and again in Belgium," Grayson said.

Henshaw moved off on an errand, and Grayson set out in search of Thorpe. He noted several landmarks to guide him by, and returned to his billet, intending to try to find him the next evening.

He was successful, and by following Henshaw's instructions, soon found the unit. Thorpe was sitting in the rear portion of a house cleaning his kit in preparation for guard duty.

"You were doing that last time I saw you; are you permanently on guard?"

"Seems like it to me; sit down." Thorpe grinned at his friend.

Soon the two were in animated conversation, eager to catch up with each other's news. The visit ended with Grayson describing where his billet was situated and inviting Thorpe for tea the following Sunday. He promised to gather up as many of the others as he could.

Sunday arrived and Thorpe made his return visit. "Put your rifle in the corner, take off your coat, and pretend you're at home." Vincent grinned.

"It's nice to get back to the battalion again and to see you all....."

"...Still alive." Copplestone interrupted with a laugh. "We're all agreed it's a good habit to get into, to remain alive; we've learnt that much."

"There's no doubt you've been lucky so far. I hope you come through the lot," Thorpe said with sincerity.

"Hold your breath, there's another VI coming. Any one of those boys can put paid to a promising career," Vincent said.

The bomb zoomed on its way overhead. Thorpe was told of the VI which had dropped in Tilburg two weeks ago, when six civilians had been killed.

Eventually the tea-table was laid, provisioned in the main with army rations. Afterwards their hosts did a Dutch folk dance in native costume, rounded off by their National Anthem. After the party broke up, as it was Sunday, Grayson and Thorpe decided to go to the Protestant Church. When they arrived a 'song-service' was in progress, with the troops calling out their favourite hymns to be sung.

Afterwards, in a nearby canteen, Grayson

reminded Thorpe that the last time they met he was about to be brought up to date with the doings of Hilary. But Thorpe was not anxious to re-open the subject of Hilary, and went so far as to request Grayson - in the politest possible way - not to broach the subject again. By way of sugaring the pill he explained, "You see the Hewletts write to me, but purely as friends. They wouldn't do that if they didn't trust me, would they?"

"I see what you mean," Grayson nodded his head and let the subject drop. In the street outside they shook hands and took their leave, going their different ways.

The division moved that week, and their stay in Tilburg terminated in the early hours of a February morning. They moved in broad moonlight, and the whole town was there to see them off. The stolid Dutchman, whom Vincent had initially won over with a cup of tea, was as emotional as the rest.

The order to mount trucks was given and the civilians stood back, waiting, the moonlight shining on their set, white faces. Spottiswoode swung into the middle of the street, followed by Grayson and Crabtree.

"Goodbye, goodbye." sounded from both Dutch and British throats, then all was lost amid the clatter of tracks and tyres on the cobbled streets.

The column kept up a steady pace, and long before the moon had disappeared, Vincent and the others in the rear of the truck, having mentally handed over responsibility for their journey to the driver alone, fell asleep.

Nijmegen. That's where dawn found them once more. Soon they found themselves housed in barracks, which judging by the pictures on the walls had been recently occupied by the Germans. Here they spent twenty four hours awaiting fresh orders. Towards evening on the second day, Crabtree came up with the information that they might move that night - failing that, then they would be there for a fortnight.

"It appears the advance has been slowed down by mud, there's oceans of it; to say nothing of a mass of minefields and booby-traps," Crabtree quoted knowledgeably.

"How far's the advance got?" someone asked.

"Into the northern end of the Siegfried Line," Crabtree said.

Half an hour later the 'fortnight' theory went for a Burton. "We're going into the line tonight," an N.C.O. said.

This statement was received in stony silence. Nonetheless it was true, and with the darkness settling over Nijmegen they set off once more.

"Be very careful to keep to the road; it's been cleared of mines," the N.C.O. said.

Hour after hour they bumped through anti-tank ditches and entanglements. Bulldozers had hastily filled in the large ditches, but the road surface had been badly knocked about. Grimly Grayson riveted his eyes on Crabtree's tail light, as the whole line of vehicles to the front swayed up and down, like a convoy of ships in a heavy swell, while all around the darkness hid from view the booby-traps which would spell certain death to any unfortunate who might miss the road. About midnight they turned onto a narrow lane, currently a quagmire, which they finally negotiated after a skidding match of its full length.

Substantial gunfire flared up all around them.

A figure stepped out of the darkness.

"Spottiswoode." Grayson's eyes were like a cat's in the dark. "Where did you come from?"

"Advance party from Nijmegen. We drivers are remaining here with the trucks. The platoons are moving forward on foot."

"The same old raz-a-ma-taz. I'm glad I'm a driver," Grayson said. "How far is the front line?"

"Perhaps two miles. The mud is dreadful."

The platoons quickly de-bussed. Ammunition, weapons and kit, all had to be manhandled forward. Glumly the drivers watched their mates file off into the darkness. Then they set about parking their vehicles under cover of some farm buildings, and attempted to bed down in a barn. Later that night sustained gunfire aroused them from their slumbers. They crept to the door and

150

in the dawn light the scene which caught their eyes was mindboggling...Row upon row of guns filled the fields round about and lined all the visible hedgerows. All belched flame and smoke; the din was quite overpowering.

"Heavy attack going in on the Canadian front; our company's holding the line only," Spottiswoode said.

"I'm sure glad we're not on the receiving end of those babies," Hilton laughed nervously.

Throughout the whole of the next day the roar of gunfire never eased. Their barn developed a constant shake through vibration. Several drivers began to build a barricade for themselves, with pieces of wood, inside the barn.

"Getting scared?" someone laughed.

The barricade was strengthened with ration boxes and bricks. As the tempo of the barrage increased, so the trembling of the barn worsened. Finally, throwing their pride to the wind, the drivers who'd originally ridiculed the barricade joined their mates behind it.

"It's a poor show when we're more scared of our own guns than Jerry's," Spottiswoode cracked.

By the time the guns moved forward and the drivers were able to rejoin their company, they were, to say the least, nerve shattered. The company itself had been fortunate in having sustained no casualties, though it had to endure considerable cold and exposure.

On the move again they detoured, which took them a night and a day. Then they halted long enough to snatch a few hours sleep. At the crack of dawn they headed for their objective, a corner of a large wood covering some high ground. They reached its edge without incident, skirted its fringe, swept its depths with machine-gun fire, ploughed through several muddy fields which formed a gap in the wood, then came under fire from self-propelled guns and mortars which brought them to an abrupt halt. Hilton's platoon, in the lead, dug-in under a clump of trees to the accompaniment of some 'moaning-minnies.' For a while chaos reigned, while drivers sought to bring vehicles under cover of trees without careering into the middle of furiously digging men.

Two superb shots from a tank put both enemy self-propelled guns out of action. Several men became casualties, and were evacuated at great personal risk to their mates, who jumped into the open to assist them to a truck.

Meanwhile, further back in the halted column, the platoons were taking their share of punishment. Each section took cover as the hail of mortars relentlessly bore down on them. Grayson, in an attempt to pass a tank, became bogged in a rut, and was in a bad way till Crabtree, seeing the danger, bravely rushed out from his shelter to direct him out of the mud sea.

A welcome lull in the firing gave them much needed respite. Hilton's platoon kept a sharp lookout for enemy movements, until the rest of the company, including the tanks, were able to move up and deploy and clear their area of the wood. The company moved forward on foot into the trees, running the gauntlet of booby-traps and mines on the ground and bullets in the air. Vincent and Copplestone were fortunate in having the cover of a bren-carrier, which effectively shielded them as they kept in its wake down a clearance in the trees. This was followed up by tanks mercilessly shelling and machine-gunning the trees with such accuracy that the enemy were seen to double out of them. A few held on tenaciously, claiming several victims among the attackers, but Oatley's platoon, with its usual dash coupled with first rate discipline, worked around them and ended their resistance with some accurate shooting. This concluded the company's task in the battle and they were then able to stand by and watch the succeeding waves of troops going into action.

With the coming of night rain fell, but no one was in a mood to complain. Fatigue demanded sleep, regardless of sodden trenches.

Next day brought no further call on them, and reports indicated that Jerry was being steadily pressed back. Mines, however, continued to be unpleasant hazards and called for the utmost caution.

The second day they moved forward again, to take over a defensive position in order to free other troops for the attack. Now that they were in a reserve role Spottiswoode was lucky enough to find a deep dug-out with logs lining both sides and roof. On further investigation they discovered several more, enough to house all the platoons.

"There's enough earth and logs covering it to stop any shell – what a find." Copplestone. said.

"Part of the Siegfried Defences," an N.C.O. pointed out.

The dug-outs possessed no luxuries, but were heaven compared with the customary slit-tench. The fact that the company was in Reserve and in such remarkably comfortable quarters had a stimulating effect on the men's morale.

"Not long now lads, we'll soon have this war over and be marching through London again, with everyone cheering us like conquerors, just as they did when we came through that day," Vincent said.

"The war's behind us; the back of it's broken. It'll all be over before we know it," Crabtree said.

Some thoughtful person hung a groundsheet over the entrance, and even rigged up a light.

"This reminds me of the time I was in the 'Glasshouse'," Crabtree chuckled.

"Then it really is like home to you." chaffed Oatley.

"Tell us about your Glasshouse experience then," several voices chimed.

Always happy to be the centre of attention, Crabtree began. "Well, it was a night just as black as this, I was driving the recreation truck and the fog was pretty thick. Old Dusty Smith was my relief. He had this notion to visit the next town while we marked time before returning to camp. Out of respect for him I agreed, and we went. Unfortunately we had a breakdown, and while we were attempting to fix it another stinking truck ran into us." He paused, as a shell landed dangerously close. "Well, when we saw the damage to our vehicle we nearly had heart failure. I knew Dusty was feeling sorry for me, as being the driver I was the one who'd cop it."

"Suppose you had a long wait in the cold?" Oatley said.

"Not as long as the blokes waiting for their transport. Talk of recreation, they were there till 0200 hours, when another truck eventually picked them up."

"So you had your laugh in the end?" chuckled Oatley, when the laughter had died down.

"Till I was marched into the guardroom next day, I was wheeled in so fast my feet didn't touch the ground," Crabtree laughed.

"Well, when you're back in 'Civvy Street you'll forget all this. You'll only remember nights like this, the good time," Vincent promised him.

The conversation continued well into the night, until a shell whining overhead brought the proceedings to a close. Like all the other places the company had found pleasant, they weren't allowed to enjoy it. After two days they moved again.

This time the column wended its way back to a rest area, with the object of preparing for later operations. They covered the same roads they had advanced along from Nijmegen, and when they halted it came as no great surprise to find themselves once more within a stone's throw of that town. Disappointment registered in their faces as they were ordered to occupy some burnt-out houses and surrounding fields which still bore the marks of a furious artillery barrage.

"What a hole; what a comedown," Vincent said.

Many heads nodded agreement.

One of the cooks found a peacock hidden in a roof. It must have been there for some time, and had plenty of corn to keep it going. It appeared to be contented but it was a complete mystery as to how it had got there.

Vincent was due for leave, so before he left for England he confidently told his friends that the next time he saw them it would be in the

'Fatherland' after the war was over.

****

"Meet a friend of mine, Phil Dugmore." Grayson introduced his comrade to the section. An old friend, he was attached to a reconnaissance unit in the area.

The dense woods in which tanks and trucks now lay camouflaged were already filling with the evening fog. Only twenty four hours previously the various battalions had hurriedly left their respective rest areas and moved forward to their present position to await the signal to cross the Rhine.

"Got any news chum?" asked Copplestone of the stranger as he handed him a mug of tea. "You recce blokes usually know all the answers."

"Zero hour for us is 0300 to-morrow, "the recce man said.

"Where are we headed?"

"Bremen ultimately."

"How long will that take, Phil?" Grayson asked.

"Not too long. The bridgehead on the other side is being rapidly expanded. They reckon we're in for a big breakthrough."

"Like the Seine crossing?"

"Exactly. A few days, a week at most will see it over." Dugmore drained his mug,

"There won't be any underground movement to help us, like there was in France and Belgium," an N.C.O. warned, cautioning against Dugmore's inference that it would be a walkover.

"In which case we'll have to shoot fast and hard. We didn't in other places for fear of involving civilians, but on their own home ground it's different," Copplestone said with unusual ferocity.

They agreed. With darkness upon them they separated to seek a few hours sleep before zero hour. The section had barely settled in before a familiar voice jarred through their slumbers – Vincent had returned from leave.

"Told you we'd wait for you before going into the attack." Copplestone ribbed.

155

Poor Vincent was frustrated in the extreme to find that when he reached the transit camp on his return the company was still on the wrong side of the Rhine.

Zero hour came all too soon. Cleaving their way through the gloom and fog, they slipped down the road to the gigantic pontoon bridge spanning the swirling waters of the Rhine, and clattered over the many pontoons which supported its massive length, and up onto the other bank where with increasing speed they headed, with considerable trepidation, into the German hinterland.

Chapter Twenty

It was V. E. Day. The day the whole world had waited and longed for.

The company was in a small village, not far from Hamburg. Six weeks had passed since their night–crossing of the Rhine. Six weeks of savage fighting, where they stormed through town after town, and outfought and outmanoeuvred the enemy through endless miles of wood.

On, ever onwards they pushed, over demolished roads, across defended waterways, till finally Jerry's resistance ended, and his guns fell silent.

So it was then that when V. E. Day dawned the company was occupying houses in a village, which miraculously had escaped the ravages of war. It was a pleasant spot, surrounded by green fields and woods resplendent in their recently acquired spring garb, under the growing warmth of a north German sun.

The war in Europe was over at last; it was good to be alive.

But the men of the company barely noticed these things, for they were totally and utterly weary. While the rest of the world rejoiced over the day, the soldiers who'd helped bring it about, still cut off from their friends at home, found the day just another ordinary day, a day of heaviness in a lighthearted world ... such are the paradoxes of life.

"Well, we came through, and it's good to be alive," Grayson said, as if trying to convince himself.

"Right. It's hard all the same to believe it's over. Who would have thought it would have ended like this?" Copplestone said.

"What did you imagine then?" grinned Vincent.

"Dunno, hard to say, but not like this." Copplestone said.

They were eating stew out of a dixie, and as they disposed of it, as they had done hundreds of times before, each man had a sombre expression as he gazed out onto the line of vehicles which filled the village street. The smell of burnt flesh and charred buildings as it wafted in over the fields, constituted a major irritant in each soldier's nostrils.

Shortly afterwards they were paraded and briefed to prepare for the journey to Berlin.

"We're in for a long occupation of this country, anything up to ten years." Crabtree said.

"God forbid; that's even worse than fighting, and I've had enough of this country anyway. We've been here six weeks too long as it is - I want to go home." Copplestone snapped.

"That's because Jerry fought so well at the last. So much for you and Dugmore agreeing to have the war over inside a week." jeered Grayson.

"What a way to spend V.E. day, cleaning rotten kit. Can't we find some variation?" moaned Copplestone.

A search revealed a radio in the house, and this was quickly connected to a vehicle battery. The combination produced sufficient volume to shake the building. The roar of a crowd in a festive mood told the listeners that London was celebrating the end of the war in Europe. The soldiers huddled around the set, their faces tense and their eyes green with envy as they heard their countr men's spontaneous cheering and merrymaking.

"Wish I was there." echoed from one mouth to the other.

"They've gone wild with delight. It'll be the same in my town too - they'll be thinking of me, I know they will," Vincent said, with a faraway look in his eyes.

"Cathedral bells." shouted Grayson, as he jumped to his feet.

Most of the main cathedrals featured in the broadcast in turn. From city to city the ringing went on ... Westminster, Lincoln, Lichfield; then suddenly the announcement... 'The bells of York Minster...'

With a burst they came pealing over the air, swelling and chiming; life-giving bells, purifying the fetid air thrown out from the rank stench of roasted cattle. Louder and louder, fuller and deeper, till the whole room vibrated with sound, and the house shook as if something had loosened in its foundations.

Indeed something had loosened, but not in the building, rather inside each weary Tommy within sound of those bells. An emotional response was set free.

"York Minster." yelled one after the other.

"Do I remember it?" Grayson shouted, his face bright with fresh hope.

"Do I too? Good old York Minster. It's V.E. Day, we're still alive, and the world is still really going somewhere." Vincent roared as he threw his webbing to the floor with a crash.

Within seconds other belts and buckles cascaded to the floor and all polishing ceased. Instead of grunts and groans, laughing and joking prevailed. Gloom vanished like magic, and regardless of whether the village possessed the means to provide for the occasion, each man donned his best khaki and went out to celebrate in any way he could. They were happy, the war was forgotten, and with freed spirits they lived again. It was only a ramble around the village, but on their return they were armed with eggs, supplied by a local farmer. But that was not all they were armed with, for they had news on an early move.

They moved soon enough; not to Berlin, but rather in the opposite direction. A second move several weeks later proved even worse, and when a third journey took them to the Rhineland, the thought of ever seeing Berlin dropped out of their minds completely.

However, true to form, they'd only just settled in when the order came through for the move to Berlin. This took place in two separate columns. the tracked vehicles were left behind to follow at a more convenient time, while the main body set out in three-tonners along the road which led to Prussia – with it went Phelps. For the first hour or so he spoke little, but as they entered the battered district of the Ruhr even his steady nerves shook at the extent of the devastation. Town after town was a shambles, each one if possible worse than the one before, with often the main road being the only cleared space through the rubble. Down this narrow gap the column hurtled, rocking from side to side through dozens of partially filled-in bomb craters, which all but blocked their path, till dust clouds filled eyes, mouths, and throats.

"What a mess. Jerry must have been mad to fight to the end like this," Phelps said to his relief driver.

"They fought like wild cats to hold us up as long as they did, when they had so little left," his mate said.

"Poor beggars, it's worse than anything I've ever seen." Phelps shook his head in disbelief.

By evening he'd seen more than enough of the devastation, so it was with relief that he drew in for the night with the rest of the convoy into a harbouring area, which lay just off the great autobahn in pleasant country on the periphery of the huge ghost area of the Ruhr.

Next day the column raced on along the autobahn with little slacking of speed, except where demolished bridges had spewed their contents across its width, necessitating considerable detours. In the main however the autobahn was remarkably intact, and Phelps enjoyed the burst of regular speed which the column was able to indulge in as it pushed on through vast stretches of seemingly endless motorway.

"There's nothing like this in England. It's a clever idea, this autobahn, to miss out all the towns and just roar through the country knowing you won't crash into anyone coming the other way," Phelps commented.

A short halt for a meal took place in the Weser valley, and afterwards they raced on through the hills to the wide open north German plain. Leaving Hanover to the right, they headed eastwards for many miles, eventually turning off the motorway and enduring several miles of rough road before coming to rest in a village not far from Brunswick.

Here they were to spend some time in final preparation for the great day, when they would take their place in the triumphal entry of the first contingent of British troops into vanquished Berlin. It was a sobering thought. Even the phlegmatic Phelps was stirred as he contemplated it, though he attempted to persuade others that he didn't really know what all the fuss was about. However, he was not going to be outdone by anyone, and when the day arrived this truck shone just as brilliantly, if not more so, than any of the others. Indeed the whole transport column, whether armoured or otherwise, glistened as if it had just come off some modern mass production line instead of the end of a bitter fighting campaign. The occupants of the vehicles were equally as impressive as they strutted about with their whitened webbing, shining brasses and polished boots, behaving for all the world like ancient knight before a tournament.

Altogether it was a brave and impressive sight which moved out of the village that grey dawn. The British soldier's basic love of pageantry asserted itself; and quite rightly so, for it was he who had helped to win the war, and was now about to claim what was rightfully his.

For the first few miles fog shrouded the autobahn, but presently it lifted, allowing the column to gain speed. They drove for several hours without interruption, when all of a sudden two rough looking figures several hundred yards in front claimed their attention.

"Russians." the relief said.

"Then we must be entering the Russian part of Germany," Phelps said excitedly.

Russians they were – just a section at a guard-post on the road. Later small groups of infantry or horsemen appeared, while the odd motor-vehicle also put in an appearance. Half-a-dozen small horse drawn hooded carts passed by, all packed with squat, dusky men and several women, some on foot. They paid scant attention to the British column as it rolled along displaying its pristine freshness.

"Well, stone the crows." Phelps said. "They're Mongolian with that yellow skin. I bet their transport never gets polished up."

Towards midday the shattered city of Magdeburg loomed large on the horizon. They entered part of it and crossed over 'Friendship Bridge', and after some further delay clapped on speed again. Woods became denser and more numerous as they flew by. Phelps noted with interest the lessening distance to Berlin, as indicated by the autobahn signs. Soon a feeling that they were drawing near to some great city possessed them. A thrill that something big in their lives was about to take place nosed its way through their veins. From every vehicle sharp eyes kept a constant vigil, looking out for landmarks which might indicate the presence of a capital city. But all such clues were missing. Heavy woods still shrouded the city from view – until with dramatic suddenness they emerged from these, to find themselves on the outskirts of Berlin. They bumped along several pot-holed roads, passed a huge burnt-out Tiger tank strewn across the centre of the road – evidence of the last bitter stand at Berlin – and drew up for a few minutes halt to adjust uniforms for the final all important phase.

They moved steadily through streets and around corners, lined in places by interested spectators; shot past the saluting-base of the military governor, and pushed on towards the centre of the city. Piles of debris predominated. Battered and burnt-out buildings met the eye on all sides.

"What a mess."

Phelps stopped short as a breath-taking sight came into view. They had turned into a wide thoroughfare which stretched as far as the eye could see, through what had obviously been the elite part of Berlin. Half-way down was a crippled tank, the turret of which, now silent, pointed at them; while at the far end a tall monument was just visible.

Slowly they moved down this boulevard, where once Hitler had driven in triumph to the sound of cheering crowds. But now it was virtually devoid of spectators. Heaps of rubble filled the areas where handsome edifices had once stood. Fire,

162

blast damage, death, and recent conflict, had left their hallmark everywhere. Roads and buildings, torn and scarred beyond repair, indicated with a vividness no words could have conveyed the terrible price Berlin had paid to remain, to the end, the proud capital of the Third Reich.

The British troops, sitting stiff and upright in their resplendent vehicles, gazed at the ruins with melancholy expressions. A number of Allied flags hung pathetically from the skeletons of many structures – tokens of welcome placed there by some citizens who obviously hailed their former foes as friends. A few miserable looking unfortunates even clapped and cheered their 'conquerors', while others wept tears of bitterness. Many others, proud of their German breeding, walked arrogantly by, indifferent to the presence of their conquerors and entirely containing any grains of self-pity which they might have felt.

But in general bewilderment was the order of the day for the survivors of Berlin. They resembled sheep without a shepherd, rocked by the tide of events which in a few short years had brought their beautiful city to its knees.

The column wheeled left, crossed a canal leading into the Spree, where each man held his nose because of the stench of burst sewers, then wended its way slowly till it came to a halt in the remains of some fly-infested barracks, which in former times must have been a superb quarter. By nightfall they were more or less settled in. Unfortunately it was warm summer weather, which did nothing to contain the fly menace. However by the end of the week many necessary repairs had been carried out, and the men were feeling a little happier about how they would fare in the future in Berlin.

One evening they had a visit from Grayson, who'd been quartered elsewhere. A lot of the time was taken up with discussion about the fearsome state of the city.

"There's no doubt Jerry got back fifty times worse than he handed out. It's not just bombs, but The Hand of God, that's judged Berlin," Grayson said.

"The Russian Zone's even worse," Rattray said.

"So you've been to the Russian Zone then?" Grayson queried, giving Rattray a look of unusual respect.

"Yes, the other day I had to drive some officers there."

"Did you see many Russians?"

"Not too many. Most of the Red Army's left Berlin," Rattray answered nonchalantly.

The fact that Rattray was the first to blaze the trail into hitherto doubtful territory had a profound effect on many of his mates – so during the next few days small parties of adventurers sallied forth each day after duty, to explore the centre of Berlin. Some went as far as the old palace, others reached the Chancellery; while everyone had a look at the Unter den Linden, the centre of which was chaos, as it was piled high with debris from other buildings, smashed fighting vehicles and burned equipment. The Tiergarten, just inside the British Zone, presented a sorry spectacle of scarred, limbless trees, or rusty weapons of war, destroyed in the last terrible fight for Berlin.

Grayson and Spottiswoode probably penetrated the farthest. Their expedition took place on a Saturday afternoon, which afforded them more time, so they kept walking on and on, into the depths of the eastern zone. For a time no one took much notice of the khaki uniform, but eventually the pair found the civilians showing an uncommon interest in them.

"Tommy?" they kept saying.

"They can't possibly have seen Tommies here yet," whispered Grayson, with some uneasiness.

"Don't fancy this, it's so dark here," Spottiswoode said, as they quickened their pace. As he spoke he looked around to see if he was being followed.

"Let's get out of here," Grayson snapped.

Again they livened their step, shot around a corner, and made for a wide space which appeared safer than the narrow alleys. A shrill whistle behind them caused them to turn, only to see a short, broad figure in a wide brimmed hat following them. He signalled to them to slow down.

"Must be a Jew. Keep going, we don't know who's watching us; but for Heavens' sake don't let them think we're scared," Spottiswoode said.

Eventually they shook their pursuer off.

"Keep going in the direction of the sun, that's west," Grayson said.

By a stroke of luck they emerged into the Unter-den-Linden. It felt safer there, so they watched Russian officers driving past receiving the salutes of their policewomen, and were somewhat embarrassed when one of the latter paid them the same compliment.

"Must think we're bloomin' officers." chuckled Spottiswoode as he returned the salute.

Notwithstanding this moment of lightness, it was two tired and nervous men who reached the British Zone and finally their billets. As soon as they'd recovered their confidence they took delight in telling their mates their story, suitably embroidered, as befitted their audience.

"You'll hardly do that again. I bet you've learnt your lesson," Crabtree said provocatively, and before they got a chance to respond said, "Well, to change the subject, we're all for the Victory Parade next week."

"What Victory parade?" Spottiswoode said, getting a vision of attempting ceremonial drill around the rubble.

"Stalin, Churchill and Truman are all coming to Potsdam for a conference, so the authorities are taking the opportunity to mount a Victory Parade," Crabtree said, lowering his voice as if he were disclosing the whereabouts of the key to the Crown Jewels.

During the next week preparation began in earnest for the Victory Parade. Both vehicles and kit were cleaned and burnished bright, and when the big day finally arrived everyone was in a high state of excitement.

This was the occasion which was to mark the climax of all Allied efforts in the west in connection with World War Two. As the parade formed up the city was bathed in sunlight. They moved off, armour, guns, soft vehicles, and men... squadron upon squadron, line upon line, from the Brandenburg Gate as far as the column called 'The Grosses Sternes', from the base of which rolled out the strains of 'Land cf Hope and Glory', played by a band of Royal Marines, resplendent in white pith helmets – sweet music to the ears of the British and Canadian troops; but utterly humbling to the spirit of the Prussian listeners. Like one man the parade stiffened, the music died, only to be followed by the boom of a gun salute. Once more the band struck up while the gigantic parade was inspected.

Meanwhile Phelps had parked his truck, along with the others, under police guard, and had dashed off to gain a place on the boulevard among the mass of khaki clad spectators who lined the footpaths of either side. He was fortunate in obtaining a place at the front, within a hundred yards of the saluting base, where he stood impatiently waiting for the 'show' to start.

He didn't have long to wait – a shattering noise of engine exhausts told him the mass of armour was on the move. Slowly at first, then faster and faster, tanks, armoured-cars, bren-carriers, search-light batteries, guns of every type, surged down the grand Charlottenburg Chaussee. The din of their engines and the grinding of the tracks drowned everything.

The sunlight flashed like fire from their gleaming bodies and wheels and transformed their shades of green and white and splashes of red into a glory and brilliance all of their own. In perfect formation they rolled by, their crews seated bolt upright, or standing motionless save to salute.

Then Phelps heard floated snatches of the tune 'Hearts of Oak', and 'A life on the Ocean Wave'. The band led, their uniforms superb in the sunlight. Steadily the marching feet, and swinging arms of this vast foot parade drew nearer. Phelps' heart hammered against his ribs with pride. The naval detachment drew abreast, and then with dramatic suddenness the seafaring music ceased, only to be replaced by a military tune - the march past of Phelps' own unit.

Until then he hadn't been sure what position his battalion had in the parade. His eyes riveted to the front, he watched with growing pride as many of his old mates came into view. A sharp command 'Eyes Right', and with a flick of their heads, they turned as one man to meet the arrogant look on the bull-dog face of Winston Churchill.

'Eyes Front', another flick, and they were past.

Phelps' eyes swam with something which was not entirely the effect of strong sunlight.

Embarrassed, he brushed them with his cuff.

"Perfect," he heard himself say.

"Who are they?" someone asked.

"Why, my crowd of course." he said.

A true Briton at heart, he wouldn't have missed the show for the world. In a terrible moment of weakness he even considered signing on again. His mind flashed back to Normandy, Belgium, and Holland. He could have sworn he saw Weatherall, Sawyer, Eversleigh, and many others no longer alive in the parade.

He remained transfixed to the spot till the whole of the marching column had passed. Then he turned and pushed his way through the throng back to his truck, for he knew that the parade was being dismissed near the place where he'd left it. He watched the battalion present arms, then the colours and escort marched off. He marvelled at the crowds of Germans who'd gathered to watch the British troops perform arms-drill. He turned his gaze away momentarily and looked at the ruins around him.

"Poor creatures," he thought, "it's tough enough being victors, but it must be a thousand times worse being losers."

The parade dismissed. The trucks filled with cheery faces of Tommies, eagerly enquiring of the drivers left behind how they had looked on the parade. And so, victorious, once again they returned to barracks.

167

The next slice of ear-pricking news was the information that 'demob' had begun.

Phelps and Cunningham, both old soldiers with a low demob group, were the first to be advised - it wouldn't be long. Shortly afterwards the battalion was advised that it was to return to the Rhineland to take up occupational duties with the old division.

"Thought we were here for the winter," Henshaw said on learning the news.

"Lucky for us we won't be, it's going to be grim. As it is you can almost buy one of the remaining houses here for a packet of cigarettes," Rattray said.

"Yep, cigarettes are the only currency now," Phelps agreed, "And at twelve marks each, they pack quite a punch."

"I heard the going rate in some places was fifty marks apiece. Black market of course, but food's so scarce only British fags'll obtain it," Cunningham said.

"Sure, there's hundreds of people outside the barracks every day, desperate to trade cameras or anything for fags - a complete racket," Rattray said, his lips clamped tight in disapproval.

"Someone even told me they're gathering grass to use as vegetable substitute," Henshaw said.

"Serves them right, they started the war," Rattray said.

"True, but put yourself in their place now; it's grim to see them....."

Their return to the Rhineland occupied the uppermost place in their thoughts during the remainder of their stay in Berlin. For the old soldiers it would probably be the last change they would have to endure before leaving the army.

On the day they took their departure from the devastated city the weather was grey and overcast. Few people watched them leave. Slowly they drove through the streets to the outskirts. Once on the autobahn they increased speed, and raced through the heavily wooded countryside out into the open plain of north Germany. They passed odd parties of Russians, but otherwise there were few signs of life. In the afternoon the

168

sun broke through. They by-passed Magdeburg, and crossed into the British zone where at top speed they headed for Hanover, which they left behind that evening. Shortly afterwards they slackened speed as they drew near the appointed harbouring area for the night. This consisted of a ring of undamaged villages, set snugly in the hills not far from Minden.

Early the following morning the column emerged from the harbouring area, with Spottiswoode in the lead, followed by Crabtree and Grayson – the old firm observing its traditional order to march. Out of sheer pride, coupled with orders to move at speed, Spottiswoode was determined to make this a memorable trip. With mounted pennant flying in the wind and engine beautifully tuned, he swept down the autobahn, his mates keeping the correct distance behind him. Mile after mile they tore on, exhilarated by the thrill of uninhibited speed. The sun dropped in the sky as they battled their way westward, through the bomb-cratered roads of the Ruhr, passing its succession of wrecked foundries, ironworks, and chimneys.

But they still had many more miles to go before they reached their destination, so after a brief respite, Spottiswoode kept the boot down and the others raced along in wild pursuit. But with the day all his, Spottiswoode called the tune and never slackened his mad pace till he reached the broad waters of the Rhine. Once across the river they covered the remaining distance with time to spare. In the twilight air the streets of the town of occupation resounded with the whining and wheezing of overworked engines belonging to the same unit which had set out from it for Berlin a month previously, and which was now so proudly returning from a never-to-be-forgotten exploit.

"We're home." laughed Spottiswoode as he slid to a halt beside his billet.

"I'm glad we've been, and I'm even more glad we're back again." Crabtree said as he stepped into the street.

There is no doubt he was not the only one who had few regrets about having been to Berlin, and even fewer about having come safely out of it again.

Chapter Twenty One

Immediately after the battalion's return from Berlin, certain changes began to affect the fortunes of a number of people.

It all began with Rattray, who was posted to divisional H.Q. at a moment's notice to his old job of driving. He was employed on special transport duties, which took him outside the unit lines. As a result he was seldom seen by his mates. Then came the demobilisation of the old soldiers, headed by Morley. On the morning of his demob, Morley, spick and span, turned up early at his friend Grayson's billet.

"Good bye and good luck," he said, stretching out his hand.

"You lucky beggar being demobbed so early, I'll be a few months yet," Grayson said.

Morley raised a half-smile at this, and his expression was one of sadness. "Dunno," he said "the funny thing is I've looked forward to this day for so long – now it's come I'm sorry. I'll miss all you mates."

"We'll miss you too, and if we don't meet, or get a chance to write, it doesn't mean we won't think of each other," Grayson said.

On that note they shook hands and parted, Morley for Blighty, Grayson for the ordinary routine of the day.

After Morley left a large group began demobilisation, and this included the incorrigible Phelps, together with Copplestone and Cunningham. Phelps and Copplestone viewed the prospect with enthusiasm, particularly the former, who had forsaken his fleeting decision in Berlin to sign on again. Copplestone, like Morley, was perhaps not so sure he was doing the right thing, but the die was cast and he did it anyway.

He said to Vincent, who was his closest mate, "We always pictured ourselves returning in glory, and marching through London with the band – but here we are going out quietly, and in small groups."

Vincent nodded.

"Not that it really matters, for we only did

our duty like thousands of others, and we'll always have the satisfaction of knowing that. None of us got decorated; we didn't want it anyway. Those who did are in a class of their own. But for us ordinary soldiers, it's enough to know that whatever bit of courage and endurance we saw in each other will stand us in good stead and keep us going through life -- I know it will."

Somewhat emotionally he said his good byes and walked off to join the rest of the embussing party.

Vincent and Henshaw returned to the fold to carry on the good work till their turn should come. Each did his best to hide from the other feelings which were not perhaps in quite such control as they would have liked. Those that were left settled down as best they could to occupation life. The billets were good, and one of these was shared by Crabtree, Spottiswoode and Grayson, who were all determined to live as quiet lives as possible for the remainder of their time in the army. Their duties in the main consisted of a succession of guards in the battalion area or on a few important buildings in the vicinity. A little sport from time to time brought some variation; otherwise life was monotonous and unsatisfying. A great reaction had set in, and frayed nerves and pent-up feelings became the order of the day.

On one such day Grayson received a letter from Thorpe, and was pleased to learn that his unit was billeted quite close to his own. He was slightly perturbed when, in the course of the letter, Thorpe mentioned that he was anxious to meet, as in all probability it would be their last chance. Grayson couldn't fathom this out at all, for it was most unlikely to be an early demob for Thorpe, as he knew that his age group was a higher one than his own.

The following Saturday, with certain misgivings, he set out in search of his friend. Within half an hour he had located him and after they had exchanged the usual greetings, Grayson updated Thorpe on their doings in Berlin. The answer to the riddle of Thorpe's letter soon became apparent when he announced that he'd been detailed for a draft.

"A draft – where to?" enquired Grayson.

Thorpe shook his head. "Dunno. Probably the Far East, one hears plenty of rumours." He attempted to raise a smile, but dismally failed to conceal the bitterness he felt.

"So that's what your letter meant." Grayson said.

"It's only to be expected for those of us in the higher demob groups. After all, unlike you, I have had limited front line experience," Thorpe said.

He fell silent, and Grayson was at a loss as to what to say. To cover his awkwardness he glanced out of the window, where he could see the Rhine flowing peacefully by, edged with well-cultivated fields on the far bank, while further back a broad belt of woods was silhouetted. Finally he said, "Let's have a walk by the river."

Thorpe responded gratefully to the suggestion, and the quiet movement of the water linked to the peaceful scenery served as a balm to his troubled soul.

"You've been unlucky recently, what with never getting a posting with your mates, and all the disappointment with Hilary," Grayson said. "But try not to worry, things'll get better, you'll see," he said comfortingly.

Thorpe stared across the river without speaking.

"Have you forgotten her now?"

"Certainly not, and what's more I hope to see her soon." Thorpe said defensively.

"How...When? I thought....."

'I've been granted leave, so I wrote and told the Hewletts and they said they'd like to see me."

"Are you going?"

"Of course I'm going?"

"Great; when do you go?"

"Next week."

"I'm very pleased for you Arthur, but I wonder if they're doing it because they're sorry for you, or for what you really want it to be?" Grayson said.

"I'm under no illusions, but I'm going anyway." Thorpe stuck out his chin and put on a stubborn expression.

They finished their walk, and felt the better for it, though whether it was the rejuvenating effect of being beside the great river or the prospect of Thorpe seeing his loved one again, neither could say. They said good bye, and Grayson stood for a minute watching the figure of his friend disappear in the fading light.

"I really hope he wins her - but I have my doubts," he said aloud.

Chapter Twenty Two

After Thorpe's departure for England life for Grayson became somewhat flat. He failed for the most part to get together with his friends, for they always appeared to be on duty at different times.

He began to spend much of his off-duty time in walking, usually by the Rhine, and usually alone. As often as not he would finish his walk by the remains of a demolished bridge which once spanned the river. Here he would alternate between looking at the desolation of the surrounding gutted buildings and the contrasting blue waters of the Rhine as it wound in and out in the course of bringing new life to the needy towns and fields along its length. There was one particularly grim looking building which caught his eye. This actually adjoined the bridge, and doubtless was once a substantial dwelling, several storeys high, but all that remained was a burnt-out shell, a stark reminder of the fact that the bridge was blown up in an attempt to halt the Allied advance.

One evening as he stood viewing the scene, a shout from the street below the bridge made him look down. To his surprise he saw a girl run out of the derelict building into the street and call shrilly to another girl, who had appeared at what remained of the doorway. Unbelievingly, Grayson watched as they called to each other, finally disappearing into the depths of the building. As he hurried back to his billet his mind was absorbed at the thought of the two girls living in such squalor, and he pondered on the harsh fact that undoubtedly millions of other Germans must be living under similar or worse conditions.

Not long after this incident a Red Shield Canteen opened in the town. This proved to be a God-send to the troops, not only in the immediate vicinity, but also to those in the surrounding areas; so much so that it became an established thing for trucks laden with men to converge on this canteen in the evenings and at week-ends,

174

where they fuelled up with tea and wads, and where many a duty-frayed soldier subsequently left with a lighter heart due to the fellowship it provided. In the course of time song-services took their place at the Sunday evening entertainment, and Grayson, who had an ear for music, took an active part in these proceedings. Out of the cross-section of men who made up the choir on these occasions, two in particular became exceptionally friendly with Grayson – Ray Borland of the Service Corps and Tom Cristie of an Artillery Regiment, and these men were to serve as useful allies to him in a certain matter.

It happened thus. One night, just as he'd left the canteen, Grayson noticed in the glare of a solitary street light, a figure staggering along under a weighty burden. As the person drew closer he noticed it was a young woman – scarcely more than a girl. It was not uncommon in these terrible post-war days in Germany to see women dragging huge parcels along the streets, for almost non-existent transport meant that food and other means of sustaining life had to be carried or dragged homewards. In this case the young girl appeared to be completely overburdened, so much so that Grayson felt compelled to go to her aid. Stepping up to her he quickly relieved her of her load, at the same time gesticulating to show her that his intention was to help and not to rob. Despite his faltering German the girl understood and obeyed his hand wave to lead on while he followed.

They crossed the dimly lit town square, turned off into a street whose charred buildings and piles of masonry echoed eerily to the sound of their feet. A light in the distance showed them the way to go. On she went, while Grayson expected her every minute to stop at some pile of debris which had once been someone's home. But she kept on walking, and when they reached the light Grayson calculated that they were about the middle of the town, and considerably off-course for his billet. He began to wish he'd not been so quick to offer his services, but at the same time he was not anxious to turn back now, as it would have appeared discourteous.

In an attempt to bring the matter to a head he said "Kaputt," recalling the word from his Tilburg days.

"Kaput," the girl repeated quietly.

"Nix gut," he said.

"Nicht gut," the girl said.

But she walked on, and as the streets became darker and narrower a fit of jitters seized Grayson. Everything was deserted. Surely no one could live here? Was she leading him into a trap, or had she genuinely lost her way? They clattered down another dark alley, made more frightening by the presence of a charred tank standing at a corner. The wind had got up and was causing its rusty, loosened plates to utter the weirdest noises.

They entered a broader street, where the darkness seemed slightly less dense. Grayson heard a sound of rushing water, and straining his eyes he saw the Rhine not fifty yards ahead. They turned onto the road which ran along its bank, and had gone only a few paces when the girl paused, mumbled a few words which meant nothing to Grayson, turned, ran up some steps and disappeared through a doorway of a tall, gutted building. He heard the sound of feminine voices from the darkness of the interior, then a match struck and a candle was lit, which threw a tiny beam of light into the night, but it was sufficient to assure Grayson of his whereabouts.

To his right, and almost on top of him, the towers rising starkly against the night, rose the remains of a bridge. He recognized it immediately and the 'house' the girl had led him to was the same one he'd seen on his evening ramble a few weeks ago. He'd scarcely recovered from his shock when the girl appeared at the doorway and beckoned to him. He lifted his burden and cautiously advanced. He reached the doorway and stumbled about, trying to find his way in, when the light of the candle revealed a small room, the walls and ceiling of which were still intact., It was devoid of any comforts apart from a stove and several pieces of scanty furniture.

Beside the stove was a girl, somewhat older

than the first. Grayson realised that these must be the two that he saw from the bridge. Slowly he entered and dropped his load on the floor – it was wood for the stove.

The older girl looked uncomfortable, but the younger pointed to a flimsy looking chair, which Grayson was glad enough to sit on after his exertions. From this vantage point he surveyed the room. Opposite the stove a sort of couch occupied a space, while a small table graced the far corner – that was all. Everything looked amazingly clean. An awkward silence ensued during which the two women glanced at each other. There was enough light for Grayson to note a measure of good breeding in their faces. The elder appeared to be about twenty-five, while the young girl was still in her teens. It was apparent from their likeness that they were sisters. It was also obvious that they were completely penniless. Their devastated expressions bore witness to their suffering. In spite of all this – or perhaps because of it – their dress was clean and their hair tidy.

"Kaput." Grayson said in embarrassment as the candle went out.

"Ja," retorted the elder sister, and opened the stove door to allow the remaining ashes to dispel some of the darkness.

Grayson decided it was time to go. Rising, he moved towards the door. At the same time he pointed to the burnt out candle; it was obvious they had no spare.

"Nix?" he enquired.

The girls shook their heads.

"To-morrow night I will bring you one," he said slowly in English. He was relieved that they appeared to understand, and rose to bow him out.

Once in the street his mind began to ask questions. Who were they? How did they end up there with no one near them? Two things were apparent to him; firstly that they were from a good family, and secondly that they understood English, even if they could not speak it.

He said nothing about the incident when he returned to his billet, feeling that if he told others of the sisters' plight, they would misconstrue his attentions.

After duties next evening he sallied forth alone to the canteen, where he purchased a couple of candles. Armed with these he set off for the derelict house. Ten minutes' walk brought him to the banks of the Rhine. The building looked deserted but a female voice responded to his knock. The younger sister ushered him in and gratefully accepted the candles. Once lit, the dingy room took on an atmosphere of cheerfulness. Grayson did not stay long, and as he was leaving the elder girl said in good English, "You come tomorrow?"

Surprised at her grasp of English, Grayson said 'yes' before he'd realised what he'd said, and made off into the night. On the way back he wondered if a third visit would be unwise. He turned it over in his mind and finally decided for better or worse that he would call again the next evening. The candle beamed a welcome as he arrived. The girls looked less distressed than before. Obviously they considered a saviour was at hand, who would not let them down.

Initially conversation was non-existent, but eventually Grayson said, "You understand English then?"

Both women nodded, and the elder said, "I speak much English, but my sister not so."

Encouraged, Grayson plied her with some questions, all relating to the state in which they now found themselves. Some she answered, while to others she either nodded or looked blank. He did manage to glean what he'd already guessed, that they were on the brink of starvation, and the contents of the tiny room were the sum total of their wealth. Finally, considering that perhaps he'd outstayed his welcome, Grayson stood up to go, when the younger girl said, "Have you a cigarette for me?"

He shook his head. "I don't smoke."

Their faces reflected their disappointment in this. A cigarette to a German at that time was of more value than gold. To smoke it deadened the hunger pangs, while to sell it produced at least eight precious marks. The cigarette racket which had so affected Berlin the previous summer had spread through the whole country, with the result that anyone who possessed cigarettes could exchange them for considerable quantities of food. Consequently in many cases out of sheer hunger, women would lower their pride in order to obtain cigarettes, and many troops took advantage of this.

It was well for the sisters that Grayson was a man of principle, and although they'd pinned their hopes on his having cigarettes, by now they knew they could trust him. Summoning their courage they smiled at him as he left. This only produced in Grayson a greater than ever appeal to his better nature to help those hapless girls.

He was still mulling over the whole problem, when next morning a letter arrived for him. It was from Thorpe. He skipped over the contents till he came to the word 'Hilary'. It went on to say he'd seen the Hewletts and Hilary, and that she was still his friend, but only his friend. She was very wrapped up in her music, and she was making a name for herself at it.

Grayson put the letter down, well pleased with the way Thorpe had obviously conducted himself. He'd behaved as Grayson knew he would -- like a real man.

Chapter Twenty Three

The cigarette racket continued apace, gradually enfolding shopkeepers and business folk into its vortex. Indeed, in some quarters, cigarettes were the only recognised currency. A man with a few English cigarettes was counted more wealthy than one with a pocketful of marks. It was difficult to escape the effects. As troops queued for meals, hungry German civilians would wander around them with their eyes glued to the ground for any signs of cigarette ends.

The agonised look in the sisters' eyes as they had begged him to bring them a few cigarettes, gnawed at Grayson – he was loath to involve himself in the black market, but at the same time he'd mentally committed himself to assisting the two girls. In his case it was for a good motive, to give and not to receive. His conscience was perfectly clear; they had to live. and the trade in cigarettes was unavoidable. Hitherto he'd never drawn a cigarette ration, but now he surprised several N.C.O.'s by taking it. Out of this ration he drew off ten cigarettes, and that same evening passed these on to the sisters. The joy in their faces and their cries of delight were reward in itself.

His initial mission accomplished, Grayson threw himself into life at the canteen, and joined his friends Borland and Christie there. But he still didn't feel inclined to tell them about the girls.

On his next visit he learned that the younger of the two was not at home. On enquiring, he discovered that she'd gone to a small town about ten miles away to have her shoes repaired.

"Why did she not get them repaired here?" He enquired.

"Because to do so we must give fifty cigarettes," was the reply.

This was shocking news. The black market was even worse than he'd imagined. However one thing was clear, the girls had no intention of demanding more from him in the cigarette line than was absolutely necessary; otherwise their request would have been for fifty cigarettes.

"Next time I'll bring you fifty, she must never go so far again," he said.

From then on each week Grayson produced his whole cigarette ration, with an occasional chocolate bar thrown in for good measure. It seemed to the girls that he was truly a fairy prince, who had the capacity to change their fortunes beyond their wildest dreams. Almost overnight they had become, in a manner of speaking, wealthy. As if by magic, food began to fill the larder and appear on the table. The stove had a constant supply of wood and it wasn't long before an oil lamp replaced the candle. Paper was obtained and the girls did a good job in papering over the scars and cracks on the walls. Altogether, thanks to Grayson's care, their status had improved out of all recognition. The provision dealer actually sought their trade, the milk vendor saw that they had an extra share.

As they relaxed in their new found freedom, the sisters began to reveal something of their identity. It appeared that they belonged to a large family who lived near Dusseldorf, in one of the towns comprising the Ruhr basin. Their father had died and their mother had married again. Their two brothers had both served in the Luftwaffe, and one had been killed in Russia. The family name was Holzer, and they had three older sisters, all married.

Of the two girls, Marie was twenty five and Veronika had just turned twenty. Marie claimed that her own husband had been killed in the last few days of the war, and that she was expecting a baby in a couple of months time, a fact which made their original plight even worse. Apart from the fact that her husband's name had been Hans Gluckmann, Marie would impart no further information. Apparently both girls had left home after a quarrel, preferring to choose poverty rather than suffer any further unpleasantness from their relatives. After some initial wanderings they'd been lucky enough to find the hovel in which Grayson discovered them. Veronika went out to work daily for a pittance while Marie kept house.

Whether their story was the whole truth or not, Grayson was unable to determine. During the course of their conversation Grayson asked if they ever wrote home.

"Yes, we write to our mother still," Marie said.

"Does she write to you?"

"Oh yes, but she will not come to see us."

"Why not?" asked the startled Grayson.

Marie screwed her face up almost beyond recognition and said a few words in German, which Grayson didn't understand. However the tone of her voice was sufficient indication of considerable bitterness towards her parent.

"We write to her that you come and help us," the girl said.

Grayson concealed a wry smile at the thought that this information would be bound to put the cat among the pigeons back at the ancestral home.

The sequel to this conversation was played out a short time later, when one evening during the course of his customary visit, he found the girls entertaining visitors all in a happy mood. He was introduced to the newcomers, a man and a woman who turned out to be their sister and brother-in-law.

"Mother has sent them to see you." Marie said.

Recovering his composure, Grayson enquired, "Do they speak English?"

"No."

It transpired that the news of Grayson's assistance towards the 'runaways' had aroused the family's curiosity to such an extent that they decided to unbend a little towards the girls and send scouts, in the shape of the sister and brother-in-law, to find out what was going on. Much of the conversation Grayson couldn't understand, but as he put two and two together he got the impression that he had passed the severe scrutiny demanded by the relations. Doubtless the 'envoys' on their return would advise the head of the family that her 'chicks' were well catered for – in fact they now enjoyed better fare than the denizens of Dusseldorf and district.

The girls' diet had now increased to such an extent they they could afford to share the odd meal with their benefactor. During the course of these meals he was compelled to drink a cup of coffee - vile tasting stuff, a by-product of malt beans, without milk and sugar. But Grayson never turned a hair, though he did wonder what some of his old mates would have done if they'd been forced to drink the stuff just to be sociable.

On these evenings Marie and Veronika were inclined to talk, the latter by now having aquired sufficient confidence and vocabulary to be a useful member of the group. When Grayson mentioned that he'd been in Berlin on one occasion, it drew a fire of questions from Marie. She revealed that she'd been there as a nurse during the worst period of the war, when the R.A.F. was bombing the city. Grayson handed her some photographs of the Victory March, and after admiring them she said that she never would have thought the day would come when she would see British soldiers marching down the Charlottenburg Chaussee.

"Never mind, it's all over now," Grayson said in an attempt at sympathy.

"Yes, but you would not like to lose the war," Veronika said.

"No" admitted Grayson, attempting to choose his words, "but you deserved to lose". he blurted out before he could stop it.

The girls glanced at each other and muttered in German.

Veronika flared back, "We ought to have won. You fought for Britain, and we fought for Deutchland."

"But we fought for right, against terrible provocation," answered Grayson, warming to his theme. "It was a clear cut fight of right against wrong, and so long as there's a God on the Throne, right must win."

"We fought for right - not you." Veronika threw back the inevitable.

"Who started the war?" Grayson probed.

At this point both Veronika's English and her stamina gave up; Marie took up the challenge.

"Yes, we started the war, but you must understand Herr Grayson, we have suffered much, we love our country."

"I don't deny that, but other countries suffered too, through your actions. Now it is your turn...You had no need to fight, nobody asked you to fight." Grayson's voice trailed off.

"Maybe, maybe not," Veronika chimed in. In a voice filled with tears she said, "But you don't understand, we have lost all, and have suffered under the Gestapo. Not all Germans are Nazi."

Grayson became increasingly interested. He was eager to hear anything she would reveal about life under the Nazi jack boot.

"You think I a Nazi? I no Nazi." Veronika repeated several times with a despairing shake of her head. "As a girl I was in the Hitler Jugend. We all were, or we had no...."

Grayson prompted, "Privileges?"

She nodded.

"Did you ever see Hitler?"

"Once," she said.

"What did you think of him?"

"He was a very great man. Such wonderful eyes; they could see inside you. You too Herr Grayson would have loved him for his eyes."

Ignoring that, Grayson said, "If Hitler could ever come back would you follow him again?"

"Yes."

There was no denying the fact that Veronika was true to type - she was a true German, a patriot of the highest order. She loved her country above all else, and whilst feeling little repentance at the distress caused to others, entertained within herself a spirit of self-pity for her own country's woes. Grayson decided the conversation was leading nowhere. All it was doing was raising old questions and opening old wounds which were better left to moulder. It was dividing them instead of helping them to understand each other. He attempted to change the subject, but Marie forestalled him.

"You see we didn't know who was Gestapo and who was not. In many ways we were kept in the dark. The Jews....." Her voice trailed off into a sob.

Grayson remained silent; when he did speak his voice came harsher than he would have wished, "Yes, you have suffered. You started the whole terrible business and it rebounded on your heads, so you suffered the worst in the end. The whole thing answers very much to 'The Great Tribulation'."

The girls attempted to repeat the word 'Tribulation', but failed dismally.

By way of explanation Grayson said, "It is described in the Bible, and it concerns the last days of the age." The girls stared at him askance. "In effect it means there is a terrible time of trouble coming. A time of wars, in which right will almost be overcome by wrong, but in the end right must win..."

"If it is worse than what we've already endured, then it will be unbearable," Marie said in her halting English.

The striking of a clock on the other side of the river told Grayson that it was time to go. He said good-bye and moved out into the night. He felt pleased that the discussion, though full of friction at times, had ended amicably and without rocking the boat of their friendship. He still felt a responsibility towards the girls, and was determined to discharge it as best he could.

It was as a result of a chance remark made by Marie one night, that he should consider varying his route to and from the house to forestall local thieves from robbing him of his precious cigarettes, that he worked out a different route back to his billet. The first part of this new route he covered at a steady run till he'd reached the haven of a light by the river bank, close to a ferry launching site. Once there Grayson felt safe, for he was then able to mingle with the crowds using the ferry, under cover of which he slid back in safety to his billet.

Chapter Twenty Four

Sometime later, on a Sunday afternoon, Grayson was all set for the evening programme at the canteen. He looked at his watch and discovered that he had a good half hour to spare before he was due at the song-service. He decided he would have just enough time in which to pay a hurried call on the sisters. He hastily collected a handful of cigarettes and set off. He arrived at the house and deposited them on the table.

The girls were in a relaxed mood, as they spent a few minutes watching the people as they gathered in family groups, and walked by the river bank. Occasionally one of the sisters would venture a remark to the other about a particularly pretty looking child, or express an opinion on a dress or other such article of clothing which some of the passers-by might be wearing.

All of a sudden their peace was shattered by a vast squeaking of wheels and the deep thud of hooves, as the rattle of a cart grew louder. Veronika rushed into the street to investigate, to shoot back into the room a short while later, uttering shriek after shriek of uncontrollable laughter. The cause of her merriment soon came into view. As Grayson peered through the space which served as a window he saw a most extraordinary looking man, riding in an ancient cart with an even older looking horse between the shafts. Veronika had already greeted the stranger, and it became clear to Grayson that not only did she know him but they were about to entertain him.

"Who is it?" he asked anxiously.

"My step-father," Marie said, looking somewhat embarrassed.

The jingle of harness ceased as the horse was secured to a railing, after which Veronika led her relation inside. He was a startling figure, with his sallow, gaunt face and sunken eyes. All this was relieved by a watery smile, which coupled with his unkempt appearance gave the impression of a down-and-out. The uneasy impression gained of the man was heightened by a certain nervousness, and the fact that he was reluctant to look any of them straight in the face - altogether a queer cove to be anybody's step-father, thought Grayson.

As he entered the room Marie gave a curt nod and muttered a word of welcome. He was most uneasy in their presence, and shuffled his feet in an awkward manner. He was introduced to Grayson and they shook hands, and after he was shown to a chair he appeared to relax sufficiently to deposit his bulging sack on the floor. With his other hand he drew an envelope out of his pocket and handed it to Marie. She tore it open, and between them the sisters perused the contents, all the time firing questions at their step-father. They did this with such intensity that Grayson began to think they'd forgotten about his presence.

Eventually Marie turned to him. "It's good my mother has sent him."

Grayson nodded an understanding.

It transpired that the sister and brother-in-law had painted such a pleasant picture of the girls' welfare that their mother had seen fit to send yet another scout to the scene, this time in the shape of her husband. This must have been quite an ordeal for him, but he had set aside his prejudice to the girls and made the journey in the only vehicle he possessed.

Grayson felt that his presence was no longer needed, so he said good-bye to Herr Grunwald and left the family to settle its differences in a not unfriendly atmosphere.

Next day the step-father returned home with a strong plea from the girls that he was to prevail on their mother to come to see them. He must have given a good report of the whole affair, for the very next Sunday a tall fair haired man called -- their brother Gottlieb. His eyes held warmth and pity, and not as they had feared, anger. He embraced both girls in turn as they clung onto each side of him, laughing and playing like babes with a parent, as he strode around the room.

For hours they talked, anxious to update each other from the day the girls had left the house in anger. The sisters opened the larder and fed this tall brother with better food than he'd seen for a long time. The meal was rounded off by Marie handing him two English cigarettes, which he greatly enjoyed, so much so that he expressed desire to meet the originator of all the sisters' luxuries. On being told that Grayson would not come that day as it was Sunday, and his day for canteen song-service duty, Gottleib's attitude -- like a child -- changed.

"Surely you do not like the Englander?" he asked curtly.

"Of course we do." they said in unison.

"You do not know them, they are cunning, they are pigs."

Veronika took up the cudgels on Grayson's behalf. "You don't know Herr Grayson, he's a good man. He's been like a brother to us." Her eyes blazed in defiance.

"You are young, you don't know what you are doing. Mother has been worried with all these soldiers about," Gottleib said.

"Herr Grayson is a true friend, he saved our lives, we shall never forget him. Mother needn't worry about us. Besides it's a bit late for her to worry." She flared her nostrils and glared at her brother.

"You are a German. You were the Englanders' enemy, but now you appear to like them more than your own countrymen," Gottleib goaded.

"Herr Grayson did more for us than you ever did." Veronika hurled back.

The remark stung Gottleib like a whiplash across the face. "So that's it." he sneered. "I suppose you love him more than me. I suppose you even entertain hopes of marrying him. I couldn't bear that."

Veronika was shocked at this, yet in a way flattered. She was mature enough to realise that her brother's words had struck a chord within her, and she couldn't deny she was very fond of the Englishman who'd been so good to them. She regarded him as a hero, and had, it is true, indulged in some mild flirtaticn. But Grayson was much older than she, and obviously had no intention of marrying her.

However, Gottleib's vitriolic and tctally unfair attack on Grayson, a man he'd never met, died down as quickly as it had sprung up, and in a short time he was talking freely again.

The purpose of his coming – to be reunited again with his sisters – had been achieved, so next morning he too left with a light heart, anxious to convey yet another viewpoint to the old matriarch in Dusseldorf.

Chapter Twenty Five

The fortnight before Christmas 1945 was one which was full of events for the battalion.

First of all Henshaw was demobilised, and his group went off with the usual absence of flourish associated by this time with 'demob drill'. In his case little bravado was necessary, as they had been told they would be home for Christmas. He said his farewells to his mates, and in particular Grayson, who assured him that he had his friendship for life. From information fed back to the battalion, he quickly settled down in 'civvy street', where he found 'Blighty' all he hoped it would be when he was finally released.

With the approach of Christmas the battalion found itself fully employed in preparations for the Christmas Dinner. In the world outside the immediate territory of the billets the civilian population also made their meagre preparations for Christmas, which to many poor souls would be the most miserable they'd ever spent, attempting to celebrate in cellars, air-raid shelters, and in the surviving portions of their homes. Weary fathers, clutching branches of fir trees, were to be seen in the streets. Children waved lighted lanterns from poles several times taller than themselves, and sang during evening processions. The Yuletide season must not pass without some attempt to make the world a brighter place.

Even the canteen was decorated with streamers and this helped to comfort men haunted by memories of home. The supervisor asked for volunteers to allow the German canteen staff a holiday on Christmas Day. So it was that Borland, Christie and Grayson, between them, washed so many cups and plates and handed out so many 'wads' that they were agreed it was worse than a three day exercise.

Meanwhile, in the darkest part of the town, that area which surrounded the remains of the bridge, preparations also went on, and with the fog and winter damp prevailing, the district looked even more desolate, with the exception of a beam of light, like a tiny island in an ocean, which defied the darkness. This, of course, came from the home of Marie and Veronika, who were also intent on doing their fair share of celebration. Grayson had been given a special invitation for Christmas Eve, and as the sisters had been so insistent about it, he couldn't help feeling that they had a surprise in store.

Accordingly he joined the noisy crowd of soldiers making their way to the centre of the town. The Minster bell had been repaired for the occasion, and although lacking its former glorious tone, its deep rhythmic strike sent waves of cheer through the night as the choir sang 'Silent Night'.

Not unnaturally Grayson's mind flashed back to Yorkshire and the Christmas of 1943. Doubtless carollers would be out all over Britain, and almost certainly Thorpe would be among them somewhere. But to the Christian, Christmas means the same no matter where it is spent, even if it happened to be in the bombed wasteland through which he was now walking. Most places would be more pleasant, but few which required a greater need to show a Christmas spirit than in the area of his own billet. His short visit would, he knew, give the sisters pleasure, and make them feel that they were part of the Christmas scene. He began to whistle a familiar tune, partly to keep his nerve up against the eeriness of the streets, and partly to give the sisters warning of his approach.

As he drew near he saw the light shining through the open door, a sure signal of welcome. Inside the fire was crackling in the stove and the little room looked spick and span. In one corner stood a Christmas tree, sparsely decorated with tinsel and candles. A number of neat packages dangled from its branches.

Marie and Veronika were in their best clothes, and both looked graceful with their hair neatly styled. After a warm greeting they lit the candles on the tree, and one by one, took down the packages. Simple gifts came out, but oh so much scrimping and saving and scouring must have gone into providing them.

Grayson's present was a German New Testament.

He was delighted, and showed his appreciation.

"You couldn't have given me a nicer present," he said.

Veronika laid the table, and the meal was nothing short of a feast, with meat and vegetables, and to round off a cake, all with the unsweetened coffee, which still required such effort to drink. How Grayson wished that he had a cup of Mrs Fenton's cocoa between his lips – but apart from that, the meal was a good one, and more than likely better than anything he would have got at home. It was obvious that the sisters had schemed and saved for the occasion, and together had spared no effort in producing a superb meal.

"This is the night we call 'Heilage Abend'," Veronika said proudly. "Tomorrow is 'Veinachten'. All our people love Heilige Abend, and even more so when they are young."

Referring to his dictionary Grayson discovered that 'Heilage Abend' meant 'Holy Night'. He thought of the carol of that name, and knew that it would live forever in his memory.

Afterwards they joined in playing several German games, till the candles on the tree had finally burned themselves out. Grayson took his farewell. and as he strode back towards his billet the church bells were still ringing – Heilage Abend was truly a night of peace. From cellars and hovels, as well as the few remaining homes, the flicker of lights indicated that each family was celebrating in its own way.

Spottiswoode and Crabtree entered the billet at the same time as Grayson.

"Well mate, this'll be your last Christmas in the army, aren't you lucky?" Crabtree slapped Grayson on the back.

"I'll not be sorry, I've had my fill of army Christmasses and a few in civvy street'll not go amiss." Grayson said.

As the old year drew to a close, Grayson had the opportunity to swap notes with his mates in the canteen about the Holzer sisters. He was to discover that Spottiswoode had been similarly helping a German household, and that Ray

Borland and Tom Christie had done their best with their chocolate ration when they saw the need. On Grayson's suggestion they agreed to team up to fight against squalor and poverty in the area of the bridge. Accordingly Christie accompanied Grayson the next time he visited the sisters. They accepted the other man readily enough, and were pleased at the pooled resources of cigarettes and chocolate.

After the usual pleasantries, Grayson asked if he could bring Ray Borland when he came again.

"Yes, yes." The girls were only too delighted. They were most impressed with the fact that none of the men smoked, and found it difficult to believe that some British soldiers didn't.

Christie was slightly hysterical when they got out of the house, and maintained that the girls were heroines, and that Grayson himself was something of a hero because of the manner in which he'd risked danger time and time again to administer to their needs.

Early in the New Year Marie's baby was born. The day before its birth Grayson met a worried looking Veronika in the town. She told him that she was concerned that she would be unable to give Marie the help she needed. After calming her down, Grayson discovered that she had managed to send a telegram to her mother, but the old lady would be unlikely to get it till after the baby was born. She then mentioned that she thought she could get hold of a nurse, but she would have to bribe her with plenty of cigarettes, and also would have to wait till nightfall before she called. She would have to run the gauntlet of the M.P.'s as it would be after curfew time. The girl had no torch, and would be very afraid.

"I'll get a torch, and meet you here in an hour's time," Grayson said. He moved off quickly back to the billet and contacted Christie, whom he knew had a torch. In a flash the other man produced a powerful torch, and handed it over to him.

Grayson grabbed it and ran all the way back to the spot he'd arranged to meet Veronika.

"Thank you so much Herr Grayson." Her voice

was trembling, and she looked worn out.

"Can I do anything else?" he asked.

She shook her head.

"You're a brave girl."

She smiled and moved off into the shadows.

Full of apprehension, Grayson made his way back to the billet.

Chapter Twenty Six

It was in the early hours of the morning when Marie's baby daughter was born. Of all the children born that day in post war ravaged Germany, she was far from the least unfortunate, having a snug room, warmth, food and clothing at hand.

The nurse had turned up, and together with Veronika had taken control of the situation. When dawn broke they were weary women, but they were happy, as their work had been successful. They would not forget that night in a hurry, nor the time during it when a knock came to the door, and the frightened Veronika threw it open, determined to fight to the death any intruder.

It was not necessary, for the stranger was Tom Christie, the donor of the torch, who out of the goodness of his heart followed this up by bringing a lamp, in case the torch battery failed.

"I was worried, I ran through the streets with this lamp. It'll last you the rest of the night," he panted as he thrust it into Veronika's hands.

Veronika was so taken aback that by the time she'd found her voice, the shy Christie had disappeared back into the night.

The nurse was impressed and delighted with the lamp, and when she heard it had been donated by a British soldier she was even more impressed.

"And I was too surprised to thank him, I'll never forgive myself for my lack of courtesy," Veronika shook her head sadly.

Meanwhile help was at hand from quite another quarter. Back in their native village the telegram had arrived, and with its arrival came the stirring of an old woman's heart. Her daughters needed her – she must go. All bitterness and pride must be discarded. Swiftly she made her way to the station to catch the daily train, which consisted entirely of waggons into which the passengers packed themselves like sardines. She survived the journey squeezed into a corner, and when she arrived at her destination set off through the winding, scarred streets of the town in an attempt to locate her children. She found them without too much difficutly, for she had memories of the river bank from years gone by. As she walked on with her loaded bag, her heart sank, the nearer she got. At last she turned the corner of the road which ran along the Rhine, and as she did so a stab of pain shot through her heart when she saw the ruined pile of rubble which shielded her daughters from the elements.

"Mother."

A voice sounded from within the rubble. A figure appeared at the doorway, uncertain. The old lady struggled up the steps.

"Veronika."

They clung to each other for a while as tears flowed. Finally Veronika half dragged the old lady into the room where Marie lay softly sobbing, her new baby aleep in her arms. Marie and her mother kissed and embraced, the past forgotten.

One look at her latest grandchild repaid Frau Grunwald for her tiring journey, while a second look around the clean little room, so well furnished and provisioned, brought a relieved smile to her face. A silent prayer of thanks to God for looking after her children rose in her heart. She remembered the day – that unhappy day when they'd left home, the day fear filled her heart. But Providence had guarded them and kept them safe, and ultimately led them to a safe refuge.

As darkness fell Veronika prepared the evening meal. Gottleib's acccount of his sisters' fare was amply borne out. The half-starved old lady paid healthy tribute to the meat and vegetables, and it all seemed like some dream to her.

Veronika had only just cleared the last remnants of the meal away when a shrill whistle cut the night air, followed by the clatter of hob-nailed boots on the cobbles. She slipped outside to return with three heavily-built soldiers in khaki, each man walking on tip-toe to avoid wakening the sleeping baby.

Once inside they all bowed respectfully towards the old lady. Frau Grunwald rose to meet them and offered her hand.

"You have been good friends to my daughters," she said, and Grayson translated for the benefit of the others.

"We are pleased to help them," he replied.

The old lady's eyes filled with tears.

Each soldier in turn inspected the baby, and despite the fact that they had to talk in whisper they were a happy gathering that night, as they rejoiced at the arrival of the baby.

They didn't linger long, and due to their number were able to stride confidently back down the dark streets without fear of attack.

"I'm glad I didn't sell my cigarettes." Grayson said.

The others agreed that their reward was contained in the happy expressions on the faces of the girls.

Chapter Twenty Seven

When Grayson arrived back at his billet that night he learnt that Vincent had called to say farewell, as it was the eve of his departure into 'civvy street'. Spottiswoode was alone in the billet, and when he told Grayson he was disappointed, for by now it was 'lights out' and there would be no opportunity to see Vincent in the morning.

Vincent slid into civvy street with little or no fuss, and was perhaps the only one of the group who made no effort thereafter to keep in touch with his friends. He would be remembered best for his ability to create or exaggerate rumours to the point of producing panic in his comrades, and also perhaps for his sheer capacity to survive every attack the company was involved in.

Not long after his departure, and as the demob date for the others grew nearer, the news filtered through that the unit was to move to Schleswig-Holstein. That evening Grayson broke the tidings to the sisters, and Veronika, who was nursing the baby, shook her head and muttered "Leben ist verganglich," – (Life is fleeting.)

"When?" gasped Marie.

"In two weeks' time," Grayson said.

The girls looked at each other, but said nothing. It was obvious they were wondering what would happen to them when their benefactors deserted them and when the precious cigarette ration ceased. Both looked indescribably sad, and Grayson for his part began to realise that his feelings for the sisters were deeper than he dared admit.

"Are Herren Christie and Borland leaving too?"

"No, but they are being demobbed soon."

The girls revealed that they'd had a letter from their brother Gottleib, and that he was coming the next day. They invited the three soldiers to meet him.

Finally the elusive Gottleib put in an appearance; the train had been late. Marie introduced him to the three men, at whom he smiled pleasantly enough, and entered into conversation, for a time dominating it. He boasted of his service in the Luftwaffe in Russia and Holland, where he'd shot down seven allied planes. He'd also served in bombers, and even taken part in raids over Britain. He'd been shot down twice, and had received several superficial wounds. For these exploits he'd earned five decorations, one of which had been awarded for gallantry during the bombing of Belgrade.

"What, you bombed Belgrade?" Grayson said in anger.

Gottleib nodded.

"There was considerable resentment in Britain over that." Grayson snapped.

"It was an order." Gottleib shrugged his shoulders.

Grayson felt it better to drop the subject, and Veronika, in her timely manner, ushered them to the table.

The conversation continued with Gottleib becoming verbose about Germany's right to start the war, and the tragedy that she didn't win it. The Tommies challenged this attitude, and each in his own way put across the point that the side of right was always the winning side.

Veronika cleared the table.

With an intense look on his face Grayson said, "It's now about ten months since we cross the Rhine, and I well remember how full of fear we were, and how determined we were to shoot first and ask questions afterwards. Now here we are helping Germans, and glad to be able to - why? Because we have seen the destruction in your country, and it is now the cause of right to forget the fighting and do whatever we can to help."

Gottleib glared towards his young sister, who'd taken up some needlework, gave an irritated shrug as if to dismiss the conversation, and went over and started to rock the baby's pram in an attempt to control the child's cries. Realisng that the argument had wakened the baby, the soldiers bade farewell and oozed out into the night.

Although Gottleib had not been obvious in his agreement with the soldiers, he admitted to Marie before he left the next day that he liked them, and they'd helped to change his attitude towards some 'Englanders'.

After he left Marie confided in her sister a matter which she had seen fit to withhold from her brother – the question of the baby's baptism.

"What will you call her?" Veronika asked.

"Imgard," Marie said without hesitation; it was the name of her favourite aunt.

Veronika smiled her approval.

"About the Godparents," Marie said. "You Veronika, are to be the Godmother, and..." she paused, "Herr Grayson the Godfather..."

Veronika clapped her hands in approval. Then she said, "Perhaps he will not like to be."

"It's possible, nevertheless he's the one who's done the most for both baby and us."

They sat for a while and discussed the wisdom of asking Grayson to be Godfather. Finally they agreed to tackle him on his next visit.

At first he was doubtful, wondering what other people would think. However, after giving it some thought he agreed. He was flattered at their obvious regard for him, and accepted the honour in the spirit it was obviously meant. Marie was to arrange for a pastor from a nearby church to call the following Sunday to perform the ceremony.

Grayson spent a fair part of the day before in polishing his kit, and it was one smart soldier who turned up that Sunday afternoon. But all his efforts were in vain, for when he got to the house he discovered that the baby had been baptised that morning in the church. His name had been given to the priest, and was entered in the records as the child's Godfather.

So it was then that Grayson became the Godparent of the child of a former enemy.

If Marie had delayed the ceremony any later Grayson would not have been able to put in an appearance because of the river. "It floods every year," Marie had told him one night, as she pointed to a mark on the wall of the room, nearly as high as the door. The prospect of a similar occurrence this year was not pleasant. What could they possibly do to prepare for it?

Where would they move to with the baby if the situation demanded it?

Two days after Imgard's baptism the worst happened. A warning came from the river police to the effect that the Moselle was rising, and the Rhine would surely follow. With worried looks the police patrolled the bank ceaselessly, removing everything perishable to a safe distance. At the same time they advised people on both sides of the river to prepare to leave their homes.

The rate of the river's flow began to increase drastically, and was sufficient to reduce the speed of any up-stream traffic to a snail's pace, whilst anything coming down-stream was whirled along with tremendous impetus. The launches continued to ply to and fro, from bank to bank, though in mid-stream each was compelled to take a drastic turn in order to head into the oncoming current, which swept them relentlessly far beyond their normal landing stages.

By the third evening Veronika judged the river to be over twenty feet above its normal height. Occasionally branches of trees would be swept past. The landing-stages rose to a great height, till eventually they towered above the road on either bank. Finally the launches ceased their work altogether, thus bringing all river traffic to a standstill.

The change of the river's height was so sudden that one evening, during the period Grayson was in the sisters' home, it rose so quickly that by the time he was due to leave the street was covered with water. He peered into the darkness and driving rain and saw the sheet of water which now stretched across the road, and even up to the steps of the house itself.

"Oh dear, it'll be through the door by morning." groaned Marie.

"Don't worry, God'll help," Grayson said as he leapt off the steps onto a dry patch, guided by Veronika with the aid of the lamp. They made their way to the ruins of the bridge. As he followed, jumping from island to island in the flooded roadway, a rat, evidently in the same predicament, dropped onto Veronika's shoulder;

the only safe landing-place. It steadied itself before leaping off into the darkness again in a frantic attempt to escape drowning. Veronika gave a shriek, but continued on her way without wavering. "You must go up there," she shouted above the noise of the water. Grayson followed her finger -- some German writing on the remains of a sign-post, just visible, showed it to be an alley still uncleared of mines. He had little choice in the matter; to brave it or risk drowning.

He shouted a quick 'Good night' and set off, feeling his way past wire and piled-up debris. Fortunately he'd only about fifty yards to go before he reached the end of the danger zone and lost little time in getting back to his billet.

All next day the waters kept rising...that Sunday night the Rhine was an awe-inspiring sight. Despite his usual appointment at the canteen Grayson couldn't resist running along to see the spectacle. From the remains of the bridge the river looked to be over half a mile wide, a roaring torrent, swirling and tearing along in its determination to reach the sea. The mass of grey water, broken here and there by writhing eddies, was frightening in its intensity. The water foamed around the ruined houses along each bank - the Rhine was certainly in one of it wilder moods, and this madness refused to be contained.

With his mental recce still fresh in his brain, Grayson hurried back to the canteen where Christie and Borland, with the others, were preparing for the evening meeting.

"Breathe a prayer for the girls," he whispered. "They'll have to pull out if the river rises any more."

The canteen was packed with damp khaki figures, as they swarmed in for their share of tea and wads. Amid the rattle of crockery the hymn-singing grew louder. A brace of cornets and several horns added to the din. Christie and Borland, the mainstays of the team, were beginning to wilt after half an hour's non-stop singing. Inside the canteen was the warmest and certainly the driest place for miles around.

As for the sisters, they dared not sleep. All

through the long night the river surged past their dwelling, as if determined to snatch the hard-won little place of refuge from them and engulf it. In the dim morning light Marie looked through the doorway at the unbroken sheet of water moving past.

"I think it has stopped rising." she cried, relief clear in her voice.

Veronika came to the doorway and together they studied the river. Marie pointed to the steps leading to their door – the river had reached the third from the top.

"It has stopped." Veronika said, her eyes bright. "It was exactly that height last night."

All that day they kept their eyes riveted to the step highwater mark, but the river came no higher. At dusk Veronika decided to explore a way around the debris of the house, one which the soldiers could use that evening, for now they had been denied access by the front due to the water. With the aid of the lamp she discovered a sort of passage through the perilously piled up bricks, which threatened to collapse any moment. By this route she was able to conduct Grayson, but the others, arriving late, found no guide, so attempted an entrance across a space still uncleared of mines. They were forced to spend an unpleasant half hour in a stationary position, fearing to move in the darkness lest their next step should be their last.

That night the waters spent themselves, and the girls, who'd chosen to stay and fight for their little home, knew that once again God had helped them. The river subsided as quickly as it had risen, so they no longer needed to use the emergency passage from the house. Inevitably the retreating waters left their usual layer of silt over the road, and this rapidly became a quagmire.

In one way the receding of the flood could not have been better timed, for it coincided with the departure of Grayson's unit. The evening prior to the move, Grayson was given a kind of send-off by the canteen supervisor and the other members of the group, who all expected their unit to move shortly also. The only exceptions were Christie and Borland who knew they would shortly be demobbed from their present station. After it was over Grayson felt dispirited at leaving the group he'd known for such a short time, so he hurried around to the sisters for his final visit.

They were waiting for him, with the table set for a farewell meal, both dressed in their best as befitted the occasion. It was a sad meal, and all three felt close to tears. Desperately ill at ease, Grayson finally suggested a prayer. When this was over he stood up, and after looking at the sleeping baby, gave a final glance around the room which his cigarettes had helped to beautify. With an effort he moved to the door...

Her eyes streaming, Marie said, "We'll never forget you, Herr Grayson, for what you've done for us. When Irmgard grows up I shall tell her all about how you and the other English soldiers saved our lives this winter. You will always live on in our hearts, no matter what our countries might do in the future."

"I'll never forget either," Grayson struggled to control his voice. "We'll be friends for ever. We both know there's good and bad in all countries."

Poor Veronika was not so skilled at concealing her feelings as her sister. As Grayson made his way into the street, she followed him, every now and again letting out a stifled sob. The night was clear, and the moon directly overhead shed its friendly light on the now peaceful waters of the Rhine, turning them into a shimmering sheet of silver.

For a while they shared the scene, then Veronika said, "I shall always think of you, dear man, and pray for you when the moon shines on the Rhine, that's when I will particularly think of you."

Stretching on tip-toe, she flung her arms around his neck and wept as if her poor heart would break. For two pins Grayson would have cried in sympathy. Instead, with a mighty effort of will he controlled himself, looked at the moon, and at the skeletons of the buildings silhouetted in its light, then he glanced back at the river.

As her grip relaxed he turned away quickly and moved off, half running and half walking. He'd gone perhaps forty yards before he realised he'd not even said 'good-bye'.

"Auf wiedersehen." he shouted.

"Auf wiedersehen." came back the broken reply - then she was gone.

He walked back to the billet with his mind in a turmoil. No longer would he be able to take refuge in the canteen when hungry and cold, and no longer would he be able to pass a pleasant hour at the sisters' home. But his main thought was for the girls' future. Where, in all this desolation, would they find the means of sustenance after he'd gone? With these and other thoughts nagging at him he arrived back at the billet. He was glad to find Spottiswoode and Crabtree asleep, for he was in no mood for conversation. He undressed and lay down in an attempt to sleep, but the vision of the grim, sombre scene around the wrecked bridge served to haunt him till morning.

The next day brought the issuing of orders for the move, and as usual these were accompanied by characteristic abruptness and complete disregard for personal feeling.

The men gathered in the streets in a sober mood ready for the fall-in and march to the station. A few minutes before they left, Christie turned up to give Grayson a last handshake. Hurriedly Grayson up-dated him on the events of the previous evening, and asked Christie and Borland to keep an eye on the girls till they too were demobbed. Christie agreed, and there was no more time for talk, for just then the order to fall-in was given. Swiftly the roll was called, the ranks inspected, then the unit moved off: Christie's last sight of Grayson was his disappearing figure in the centre of three swinging lines of khaki, a crowd of waving Germans lining the footpaths and hanging out of windows.

They marched 'at ease' so this enabled them to return the compliments of the civilians. "Gute reisen," (Good journey) shouted a lanky, half starved youth, who was one of the many who'd benefited from cigarettes from the 'Englanders'. Handkerchieves appeared, shouting broke out, and tears began to flow down faces in the crowd.

The long lines of immaculately dressed troops, all in full marching order, couldn't help but find a response in the soldier-loving Germans. Slowly the company wound its way through the streets of the town, then moved at a steady pace towards the station, leaving little groups of sad, chattering people, some of whom lingered in the streets long after the soldiers had passed from view.

Chapter Twenty Eight

That evening, when Borland and Christie put in an appearance, the sisters looked very miserable.

"So Herr Grayson has gone," Marie said sadly.

"Yes, his battalion moved to-day," Christie replied, trying to keep his voice cheerful.

"When do you go?"

"I go within the week, but Borland will be here for a while."

Both girls looked even more depressed.

"It's bad news for us, we will miss you terribly," Marie shook her head sadly.

"All the good times will be over then. This is the best winter we've had for years," Veronika said, speaking for the first time.

"Won't you go back to your mother?" Christie asked cautiously. "Surely it would be better than staying here?"

"It's better for us here, Mother has too many in the house already," Marie said.

"This little room is our home, we can't leave it now," Veronika said.

As the two men made their way back to the billet they marvelled at the sisters' continued stubbornness. They agreed that there was an element of pride in their makeup which prevented them from returning home, in case they would be accused of burdening the rest of the family. It was clear now that the break had been made it would take a substantial reduction in the girls' pride before they would once more live under their mother's roof.

The last few days of Christie's service passed quickly enough, and his last evening was spent in calling at the canteen and with the sisters. For the final time he accompanied Borland through the streets. The night was particularly dark and gloomy, and it served as a constant reminder to him of the many Germans who still had no home. He said good bye to his friend, and they went their separate ways.

Borland remained on as the mainstay of the canteen, but he did not neglect the sisters, nor did he allow the cigarette supply to dry up. Luckily, by the time his demobilisation came along, the worst of a particularly severe winter was over, and with its ending the fight for survival eased a fraction.

In due course it was Borland's turn to say good bye to the sisters. He rocked the tiny Irmgard, who was growing fast, and returned her to Marie. As before, Veronika was reluctant to let him go, and pattered after him as he made his way up the road. Through the empty streets she kept pace with him, he in his great clumping boots and she in tiny shoes. She talked incessantly, as if by this means attempting to postpone the final parting. She followed him right to the door of the canteen.

"Good bye Veronika, I must go." he said sharply. He was embarrassed at the thought of a prolonged farewell.

"Good bye," she took his outstretched hand. With tears in her eyes she turned and ran down the street – in a moment she was gone.

With some relief Borland went into the brightly lit canteen and threw himself into the activities in an attempt to forget the plight of the girl's. He consoled himself with the knowledge that he'd done his bit for them, and he could do no more.

His demob went off without a hitch, and it was not really till the white cliffs of Dover hove into sight that he was finally able to shake off all thoughts of the sisters and to turn his mind to the thoughts of a homecoming.

Meanwhile, in a barracks in Northern Germany a group of soldiers were celebrating, for demob day had come. Among their number were Hilton, Crabtree and Spottiswoode.

"So long, all the best; keep out of the hands of the law."

"Maybe you'll make a fortune in civvy street."

These and other remarks saw the men off, for it was by far the largest group yet to go, and despite the early hour and low temperature it had attracted a large crowd from the battalion.

Oatley and Grayson stood back as the trucks began to load, wishing with all their hearts that it was their turn, but disciplining themselves not to reveal their true feelings.

"Oh well, it won't be too long now," Oatley said in an attempt at consolation.

"Blighty, here I come." shouted Hilton as the transport moved out.

A frantic interchange of ribald remarks took place between those on the vehicles and the men who were comdemned to remain behind.

"Well, that's that, we're civvies now," Hilton said, as the convoy turned the corner and blotted from sight the waving men.

"I'll bet we miss 'em when we get back to Blighty, all the same." Crabtree said.

The convoy picked up speed, and a two hour drive gave way to a two hour train journey. After that came twelve hours of waiting in yet another barracks before they were able to start the final phase of their journey. By now the group had been split into smaller groups according to their ultimate destinations, and in the reshuffle Crabtree had to say farewell to Spottiswoode and Hilton. They parted company with a few mumbled words and a wink, totally inadequate for such a momentous occasion, but their expressions conveyed more than words ever could.

Crabtree finally reached home, and not a lot was heard of him thereafter. But if any of his close friends had been asked to guess what he was up to in civvy street, they doubtless would have said... "If any of you see a bloke with a red handkerchief tied around his neck and with his cap in the reversed position, driving an eight-wheeler, somewhere in the North Midlands, then a pound to a penny that's Crabtree."

Both the others had a smooth trip home. The third phase of the journey, which began at midnight, went smoothly enough, and they were awakened by the morning light streaming through the windows of the railway-carriage. For a while they travelled through pleasant enough country, but later that day they found themselves moving through the war-ravaged districts of the Ruhr to which they needed no introduction. They were

209

steadily working their way through their haversack rations when all of a sudden the train drew up in what had once been a large town, but was now reduced to rubble. It wasn't long before a line of hungry young faces appeared along the edge of the railway track, and out of cellars and holes they poured, holding out their hands and imploring, saying over and over again, "Kamerad, haven sie nicht brod?" – (comrade, have you any bread?)

Their faces, though only of children, were old beyond their years, and their expressions were unbelievably gaunt. The ravages of war had reduced these youngsters to nothing short of hyenas. The soldiers threw out of the windows what they could spare of their rations and these pieces were soon torn apart. The men were grateful when the train moved on, but after half an hour it halted again and a similar scene was repeated.

"At least we know we'll get a feed sometime, it's more than those poor beggars can look forward to," Spottiswoode said.

That evening they crossed the Rhine.

"What a lot has happened to us since we first crossed this," Hilton said, as he gazed down into the muddy waters.

Later that night they passed through Tilburg, a much brighter place than the town in which they'd sought refuge from cold and the strain of campaigning.

Brussels was reached in the early hours of the morning. It was as unlike the city they'd helped liberate nearly eighteen months ago as it was possible to be.

Tournai was the next stopping place. Here they remained for twenty four hours before crossing the channel. Ultimately they reached London, and were let loose in civvy street.

Meanwhile Oatley and Grayson had another four weeks to wait. It seemed to them that their time would never come, but it did, and with their departure for England, 'the old firm' came to an end. During the closing weeks of their service, these two, who were normally poles apart,

210

reached a rare understanding with each other.

"You know old lad, there was a time when I used to think you were a 'sissy', and your chapel mates too. But I've come to respect you," Oatley said to Grayson one evening. "We're the only two left out of the Yorkshire crowd, and I fully agree with you that right must win – we've seen it come true." Oatley added.

Grayson was aware that for Oatley, a confirmed atheist, to have said as much as he did, was a rare compliment.

"Atheist or not, I've learned to admire you too, for you've proved yourself to be every inch a soldier." Grayson replied.

They exchanged addresses, and promised to keep in touch. Grayson did just that, for several months later, when he was in Oatley's part of London, he called at the house, only to be told by his parents that Oatley had joined the Metropolitan Police.

Yet another place was at the top of Grayson's visiting list.

One beautiful day in late summer he found himself at York railway station. Not without sentiment he gazed at the Minster, as he got a mental flash-back of the day the battalion departed for Normandy two years before.

Several hours later he was the centre of an admiring group in the Fenton household. Everything was the same, just as he'd left it – even the cocoa – when it put in an appearance at supper time.

How they all talked -- everyone wanted to know all that had happened. It was just like coming home, and the next day when he called on the Hewletts the same process was repeated. He was forced to sit down and answer all the questions which had been stored up since they saw him last.

"I told you God would bring us back," he said quietly, turning to Hilary, who looked as graceful as ever.

She nodded, and glanced in Ruth's direction.

"Yes, we hadn't forgotten you did," Ruth said.

As Grayson wandered down the street from the Fentons he kept meeting old acquaintances; all without exception were delighted to talk to him.

One old-timer said, "I'm going to ask you two questions, and you don't have to answer if you don't wish; what was the worst sight you ever saw, and what was the finest?"

Without a pause Grayson said, "The Spud Patch' incident was the worst, and the liberation of Brussels was the finest."

Naturally he had to explain the meaning of the Spud Patch and all the attack implied.

"What do you think of Jerry, now that you've met 'im?" another old man asked.

"He's tough," Grayson said.

"Aye, 'es tough." agreed the old fellow.

When he got the length of Aunt Elizabeth he found her sitting in the kitchen humming to herself. She looked not a day older than the day she'd waved them off. She gave him a great welcome.

"I'm glad to see you too, Granny," Grayson said, as he shook hands with the rest of her family.

She pointed him to a chair, and when he'd made himself comfortable she said. "Well, what was it like?"

"Terrible Granny, many times I wondered if any of us would come back at all."

"I prayed for you every night," she said, her eyes bright.

"I knew you would, and that's why I'm here now." Grayson smiled his slow smile.

The old lady called to her daughter to bring some magazines, which she'd kept specially for the occasion.

"Are these your unit?" she asked hopefully, pointing to some battle pictures.

He shook his head. "We were quite near there," he admitted.

"It must all have been terrible," she said as she scanned the pages.

"Like The Great Tribulation," he said, "all that we went through, and what we witnessed others suffer, definitely had a spiritual significance."

At that Aunt Elizabeth frowned in perplexity.

212

It was obvious she didn't attach the same interpretation to the war as he had done. He saw her expression and hastened to add, "At best it was a warning to us of what it'll be like."

"You must now forget it," she advised, and looked at him with motherly sympathy.

"I only wish I could, but I cannot forget; nor can I forget my mates, or my friends in Germany."

"Friends in Germany?" she retorted with surprise.

"Yes."

"You were fighting them only a short while ago, now you talk of having friends among them?" She looked at him in puzzlement.

"We fed them when we found they were starving, after the fighting was done," he said simply.

"Ah," she smiled her understanding, "then that's the way right wins..... love your enemies."

"That is so," he said, pleased with her simple summing up of the matter. "In battle or trouble I've noticed both good and bad are involved, but in the end only good really wins. Good men, by doing right, lose nothing whether they live or die..." he said.

"You mean that's a good example of how we all should live. You remember your friend; what was his name?" she said.

"Thorpe?"

"Aye that's him. Well he was here some time ago, and when he came he hardly spoke a word. We all knew what he was thinking. Hilary's a grand girl, and he took it hard when she made her decision."

Grayson nodded slowly in understanding.

"Well, we heard from him some days ago, from the Middle East. He seems lonely, but he's putting a brave face on it. I admire him very much," the old lady said. "Taking disappointment is part of fighting for right."

Later that afternoon Grayson started off back down the road to the village. As he puffed up the hill, he saw the seat just ahead of him. When he drew close he noticed it was missing several planks and was rotting in the middle.

For a moment he stopped, and thought about old memories as they crowded in on him. A distant rattling and the strident scream of a whistle brought him out of his reverie.

He turned in the direction of the sound and was just in time to see 'The Flyer' on its evening run from York burst into view.

"It's good to see you again, old lad," he muttered as the train snorted past. "I'm glad nothing has changed in this part of the world." he said to himself.

On reaching the Fenton household, Clare handed him a letter which had been forwarded from his home. He made his way to his room, as he wanted some privacy in which to read it. He glanced at the signature and recognized Borland's writing.

He began to read. Within seconds his eye caught a sentence – 'I'm very sorry to have to tell you that our little supervisor, and leader of the canteen, has been killed in an accident. I only learnt yesterday, so have written to you at once as I know how badly you will feel about it.....'

For a moment Grayson was speechless, shocked to his very core. He dropped the letter and paced about the room in an attempt to control his thoughts. Finally he paused in front of the open window and gazed across the valley. He drank in the scene for perhaps five minutes.

Eventually he turned and murmured softly to himself, "Once again it's been proved, the good as well as the bad go down – but she has won, for as sure as night follows day, she's gone to Heaven."